CW00433695

Computers

Right from the Start

2nd Edition

By R.P. Richards

Published by

PAYNE-GALLWAY
PUBLISHERS LTD
26-28 Northgate Street, Ipswich IP1 3DB
Tel: 01473 251097 • Fax: 01473 232758
www.payne-gallway.co.uk

Acknowledgements

Payne-Gallway is a division of Harcourt Education Ltd.

Linacre House
Jordan Hill
Oxford
OX2 8DP

Second Edition 2005

08 07 06 05
10 9 8 7 6 5 4 3 2 1

ISBN 1 904467 83 0

British Library Cataloguing in Publication data is available from the British Library on request

Printed in Malta by

Gutenberg Press Limited

Contents

Chapter 1 – **Getting Started**	2
Chapter 2 – **Writing a Letter**	12
Chapter 3 – **Saving**	19
Chapter 4 – **Printing**	28
Chapter 5 – **Making a Poster**	33
Chapter 6 – **Household Accounts**	42
Chapter 7 – **Surfing the Internet**	56
Chapter 8 – **E-mails**	67
Chapter 9 – **More Pictures**	76
Chapter 10 – **Music on the PC**	83
Chapter 11 – **Troubleshooting**	88
Index	94

Getting Started 1

This book is for people who are new to computers – perhaps you have just bought your first home PC, or started an introductory course at college or in your workplace.

It aims to give you a 'taster' of what you can do on a PC and give you the confidence to move on and find out more.

Your computer

Your computer will have a main system unit that incorporates a hard disk drive, a CD-ROM or DVD-ROM drive, a floppy disk drive and the on/off switch. It will also have a screen, a keyboard and a mouse. In addition, most new PCs are supplied with speakers and a printer.

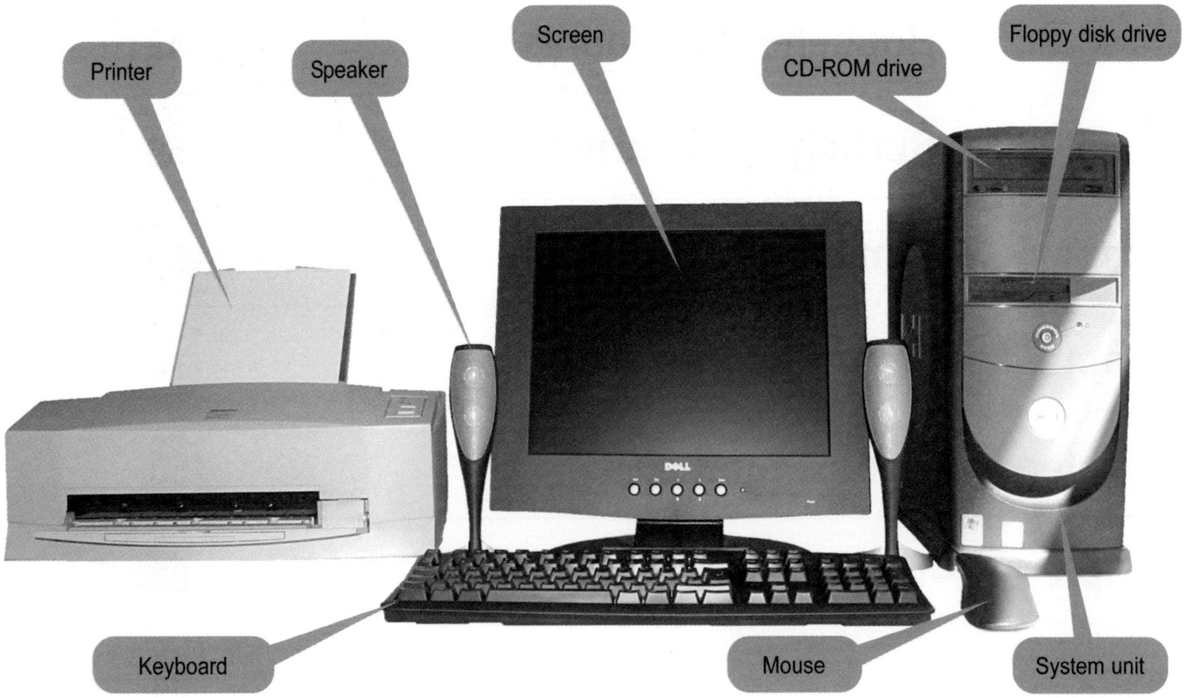

Switching on

Check that the floppy disk drive is empty and then switch on the power.

- Press the power switch on the front of the system unit. Also remember to switch on the screen and the printer.

Important: Never switch off your computer without shutting it down first - you will hear more about this later.

The system will immediately run a power-on self-test to check that everything is working OK.

Wait for the screen to stop changing. It should end up with some small symbols (called icons) and a coloured background – this is called your desktop.

Figure 1.1: The Windows XP desktop

Tip: Whenever you see a small egg-timer on your screen, your computer wants you to wait. Don't press any buttons until it goes away.

Changing the background

If you don't like the desktop background you can easily change it.

If you are not used to using the mouse, wait until you have completed the rest of this chapter then have a go.

- Right-click the mouse on the desktop picture.
- In the menu that appears, left-click the Properties option.
- This opens the Display Properties box. Click on the Desktop tab.

Tip: In Windows 2000 click the **Background** tab.

- Scroll down the list and click on a background. You will see a preview of what it looks like.
- When you find one you like, click OK.

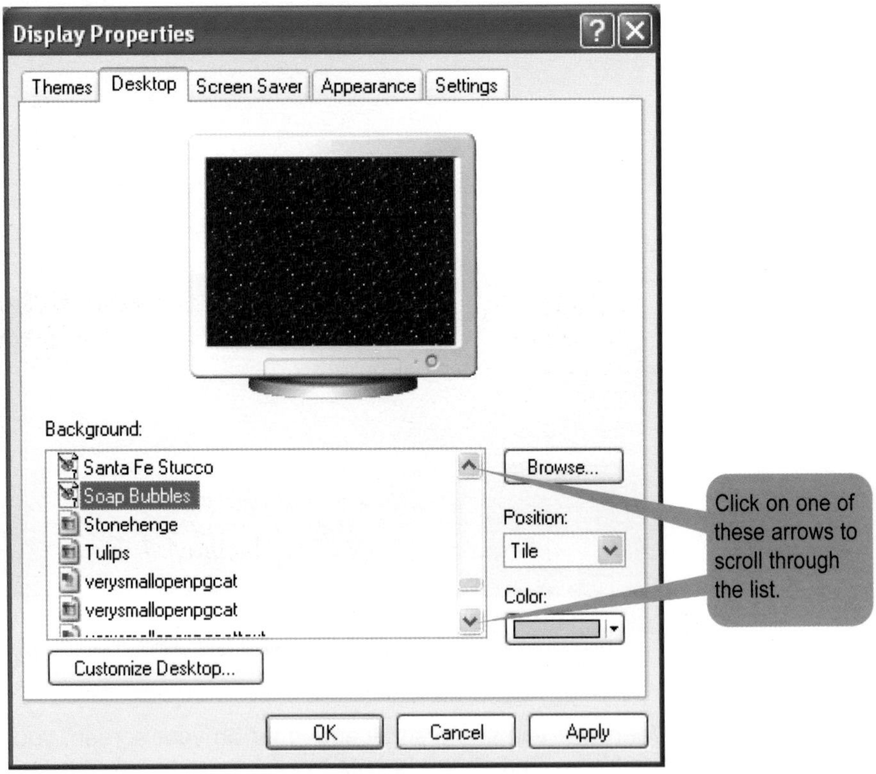

Figure 1.2

Tip: To scroll up and down a list of items, click on one of the arrows on the scroll bar.

Using the mouse

The mouse is used to give your computer instructions, and you need to learn how to control it. It's a bit like learning to ride a bicycle – once you can do it, it's easy.

- If you are right-handed then hold the mouse like this:

Tip: If your mouse has three buttons, just ignore the middle one.

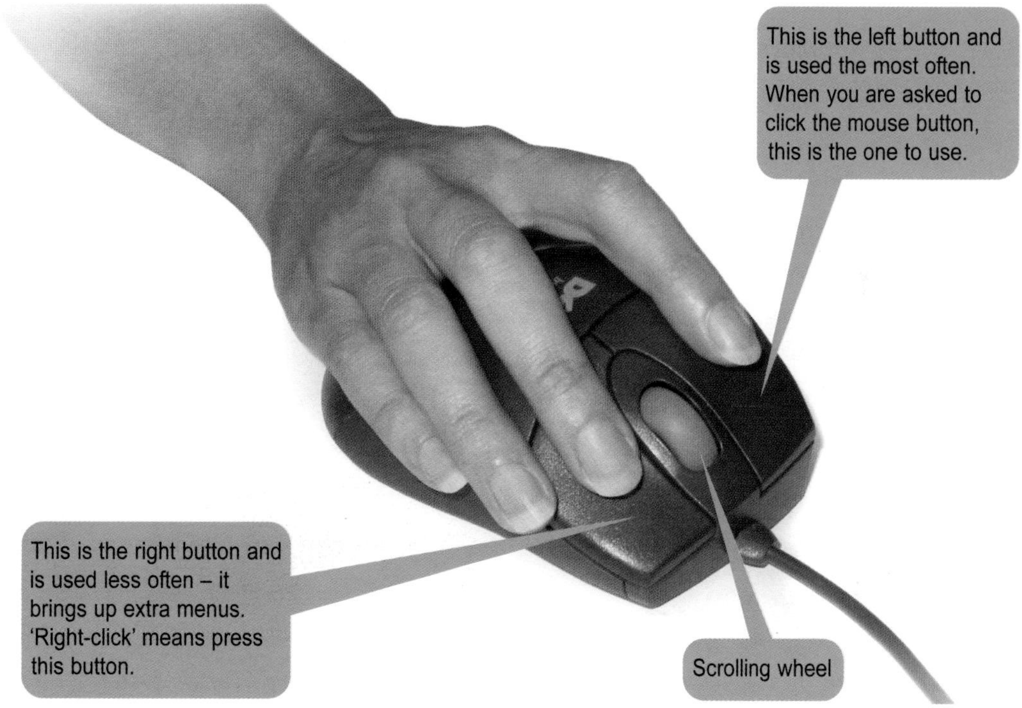
This is the left button and is used the most often. When you are asked to click the mouse button, this is the one to use.
This is the right button and is used less often – it brings up extra menus. 'Right-click' means press this button.
Scrolling wheel

Figure 1.3

Tip: Some types of mouse have a scrolling wheel (or button) – more about this later.

If you are left-handed, your index finger will be on the right button instead of the left one.

Mouse practice

- Push the mouse around. You will see that it moves an arrow-shaped pointer around the screen.
- Click the left button – you can hear it click.

We will use a games program that is supplied free with Windows to practise using the mouse.

- Move the mouse pointer so that it is positioned over the button labelled Start in the bottom left-hand corner of your screen.
- Click the left mouse button. A list will appear.
- Move the mouse pointer over All Programs and click again.
- Move the mouse pointer over the word Games and click.
- Move the pointer across to FreeCell and click again.

Tip: In Windows 2000, click **Programs**, **Accessories**, **Games**, **FreeCell**.

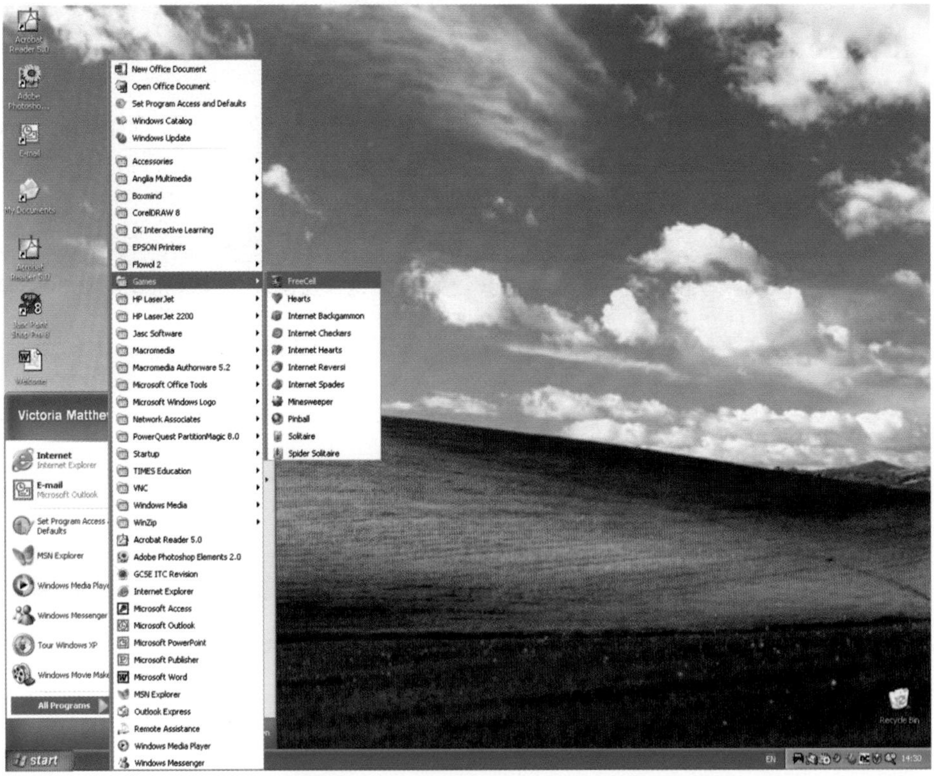

Figure 1.4: Selecting a program

Note: You will probably have a different list of programs from this.

FreeCell is a card game that you can play on the computer. When the program first starts, it will appear in a window like this.

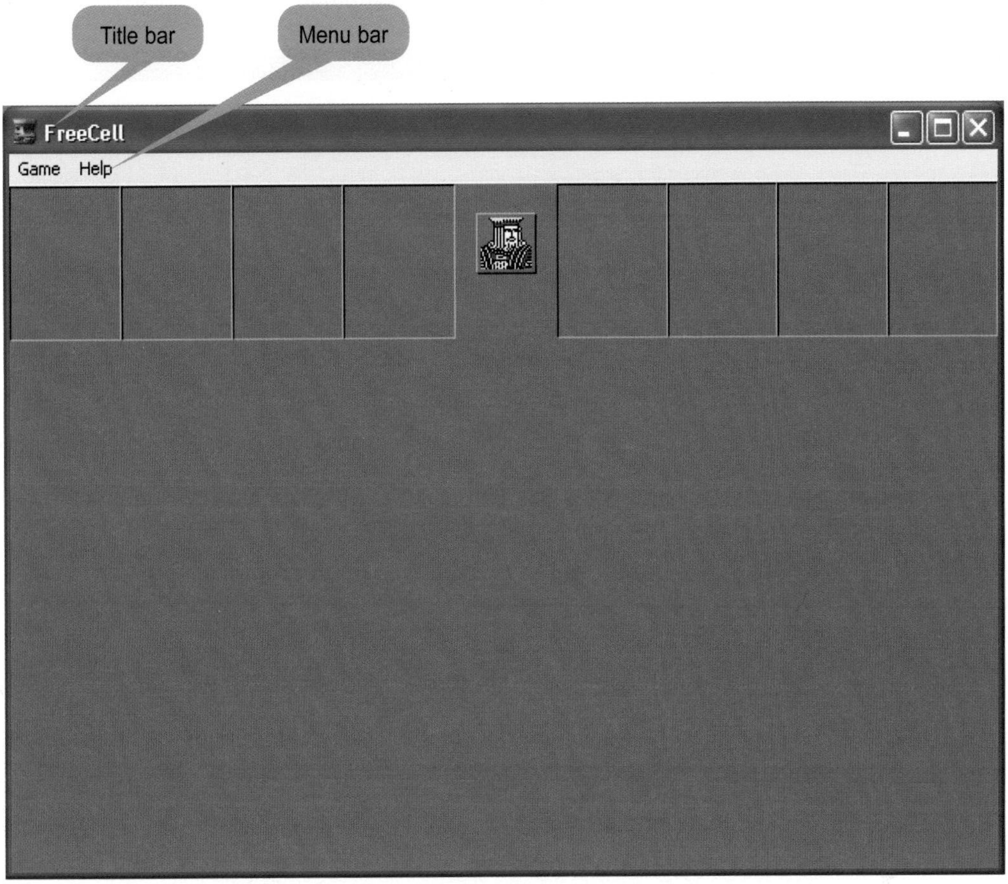

Figure 1.5: The Freecell window

The Title bar contains the title of the program (FreeCell in this case) and there are three small buttons on the right.

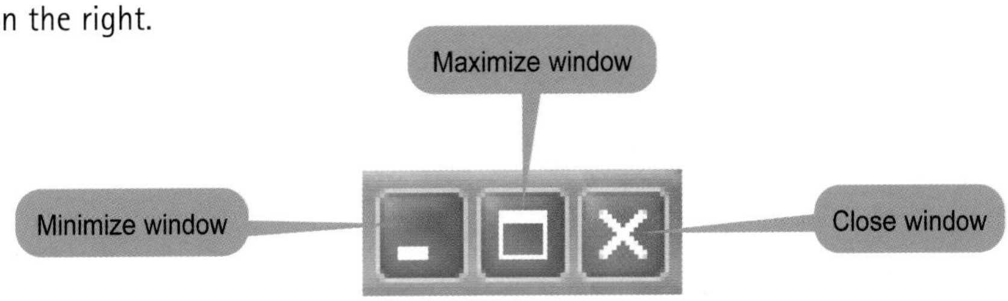

Figure 1.6: Window buttons

Tip: Hover the mouse over each button and a **Screen Tip** tells you the name of the button.

Move your mouse pointer over the Minimize button and click with the left mouse button.

Don't panic – the window disappears, but not completely. Look at the bottom of the screen and you should see a bar labelled FreeCell. This appears on the Task bar, which is a Windows feature that shows you which programs are currently running.

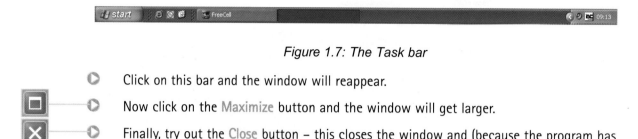

Figure 1.7: The Task bar

- Click on this bar and the window will reappear.

- Now click on the Maximize button and the window will get larger.
- Finally, try out the Close button – this closes the window and (because the program has only one window) closes the program too.

Now you are back where you started.

- Practise going back to the Start menu and opening up the FreeCell program again.

You should now have a window like Figure 1.5 on the screen. The line below the title bar is called the menu bar.

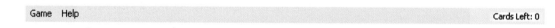

Figure 1.8: The Menu bar

This bar has labels that, when clicked, produce drop-down menus with options to choose from. Different programs will have different menus: FreeCell has only two.

- Move the mouse pointer over the word Game and click the left mouse button.

Tip: If the instructions just say click, it means click the left mouse button.

A drop-down menu like this will appear.

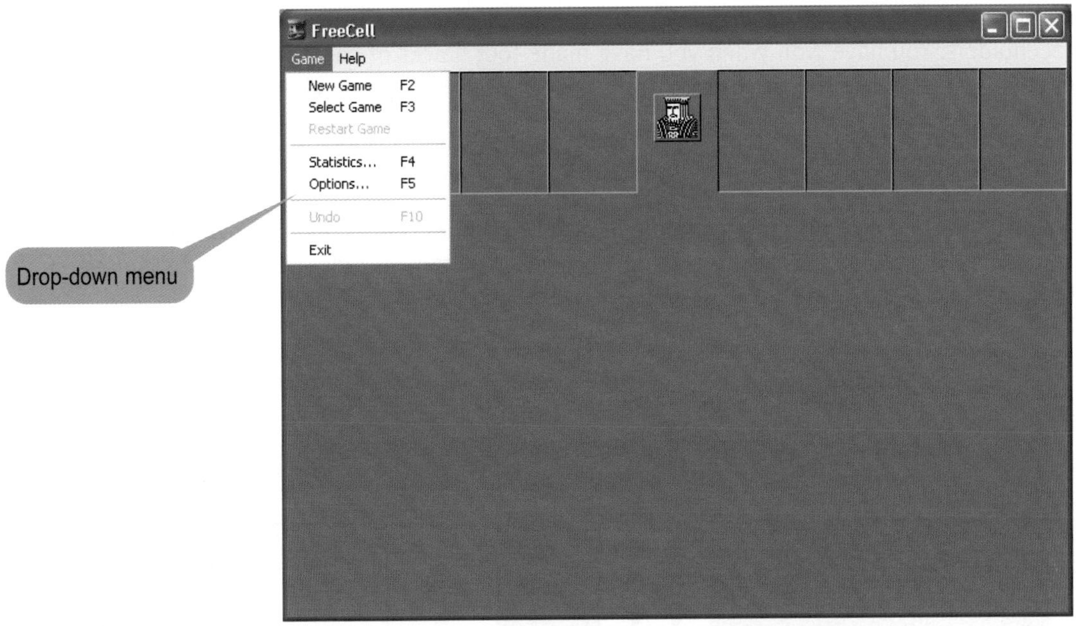

Figure 1.9: The Game menu

- Move your pointer down and click on New Game.

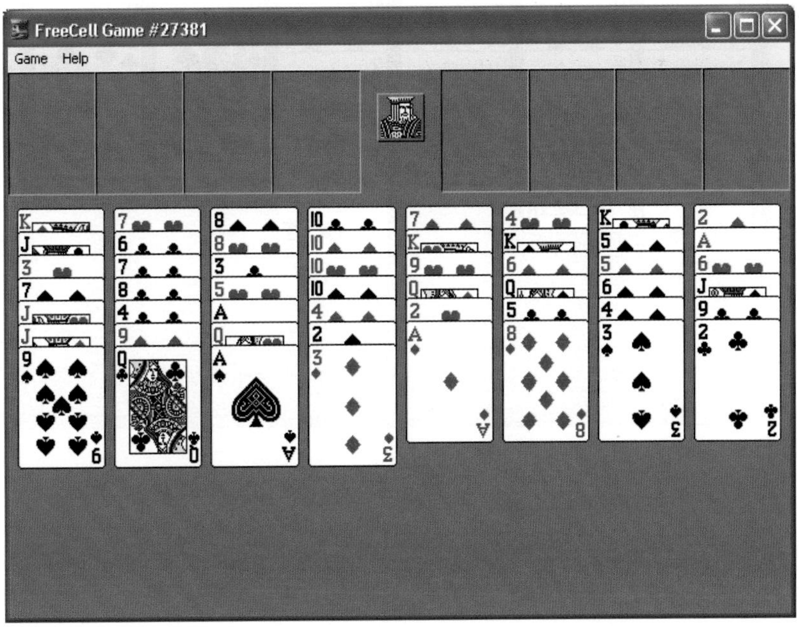

Figure 1.10: Ready to play a new game

Note: Some say that every game is winnable – but I don't believe it!

Playing the game

The object of FreeCell is to move all the cards into the home cells, using the free cells as placeholders. You have won when you have made four stacks of cards on the home cells, one for each suit, stacked in order of rank from lowest (ace) to highest (king).

- To move a card, click the card you want to move, and then click where you want to move it to. You can move cards to a different column, a free cell or a home cell.

Moves to another column must be made in order of highest card (king) to lowest (ace), in alternating suit colours. Moves to a home cell must be made in order of lowest to highest, in the same suit.

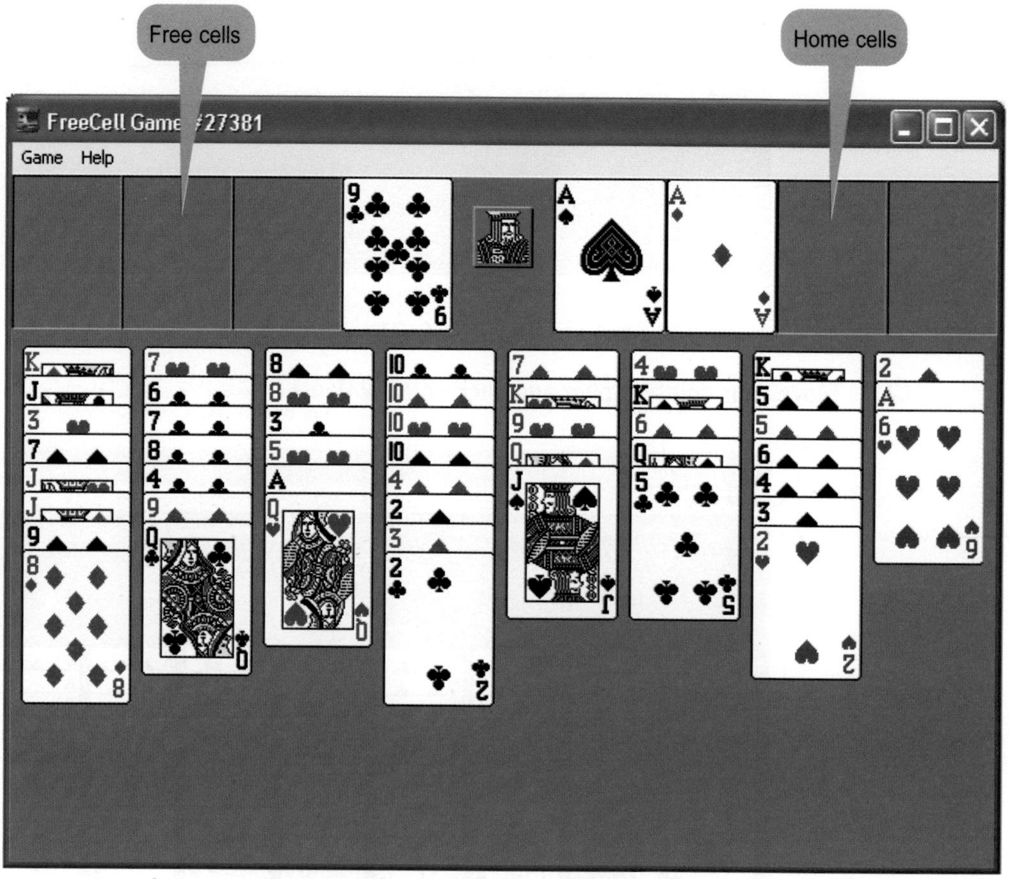

Figure 1.11: The game in progress

Tip: You can move several cards to a new column if they are stacked in order correctly.

Using Help

If you would like to get more detailed instructions on how to play FreeCell, or you want to look up recommended strategies and tips, use the Help menu. Almost all Windows programs have a Help menu and this can be invaluable if you don't have a reference book or an experienced user around to ask!

> **Tip:** You can also access the **Help** system by pressing the key labelled **F1** on the keyboard.

- Move the mouse pointer over the word Help and click with the left mouse button. Click on Contents.

A help window will appear like this.

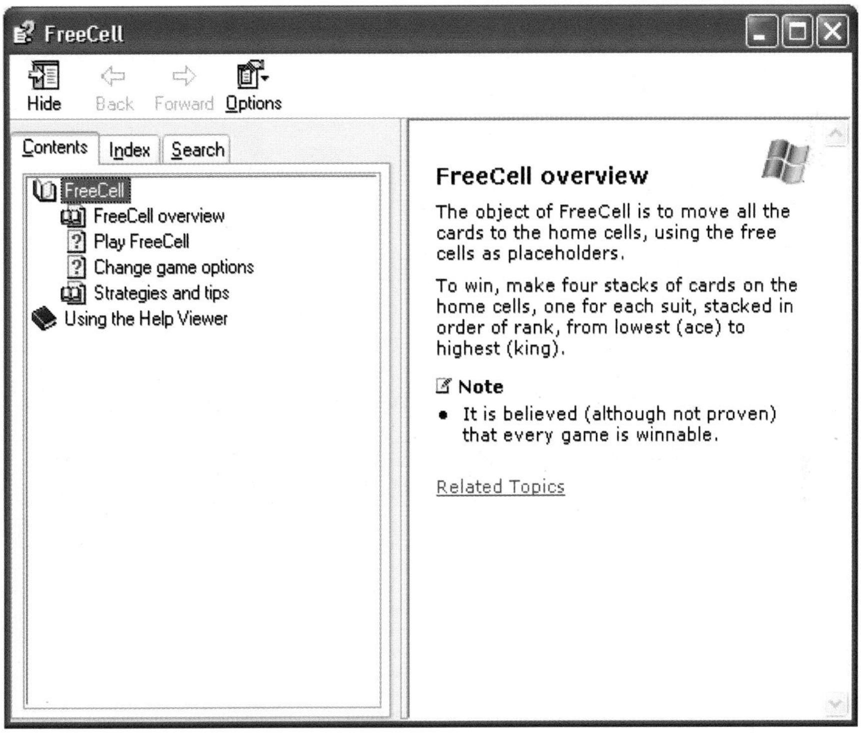
FreeCell
Hide
Back
Forward
Options
Contents
Index
Search
FreeCell
FreeCell overview
Play FreeCell
Change game options
Strategies and tips
Using the Help Viewer
FreeCell overview
The object of FreeCell is to move all the cards to the home cells, using the free cells as placeholders.
To win, make four stacks of cards on the home cells, one for each suit, stacked in order of rank, from lowest (ace) to highest (king).
Note
It is believed (although not proven) that every game is winnable.
Related Topics

Figure 1.12: The help window

- Click on one of the options in the left-hand part of the window and the information will appear on the right.

- To return to the game, click the Close window button.
- If you want to play another game, click on New Game from the Game menu.
- If you want to close FreeCell, either click on Exit from the Game menu or click the Close button.

Writing a Letter

2

A PC can be very useful for typing various kinds of documents. One of the most frequently-produced documents is a formal letter.

The software used to produce written documents is called word processing software. One of the most common word processing packages is Microsoft Word.

Opening Word

Open Word in a similar way to the FreeCell game:

- Click on Start, then move up the list to All Programs (just Programs for Windows 2000). Depending on the version you have, click Microsoft Word (for versions prior to Word 2003), or click Microsoft Office and then Microsoft Office Word 2003.

Tip: Microsoft Word is a separate product to Windows – you may not have it installed on your PC.

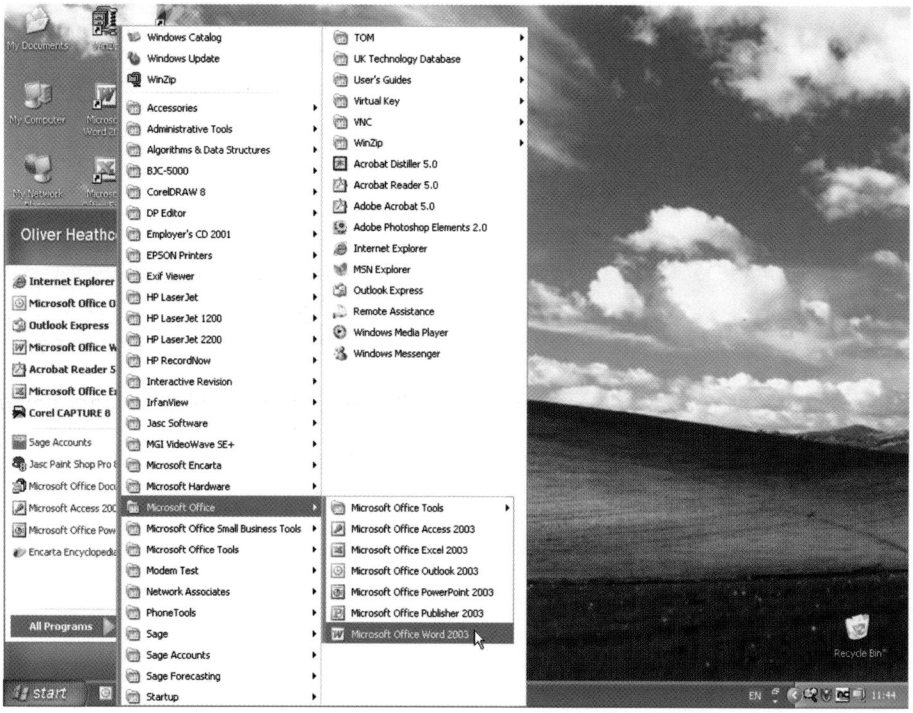

Figure 2.1: Opening Word

Word will open with a screen like this:

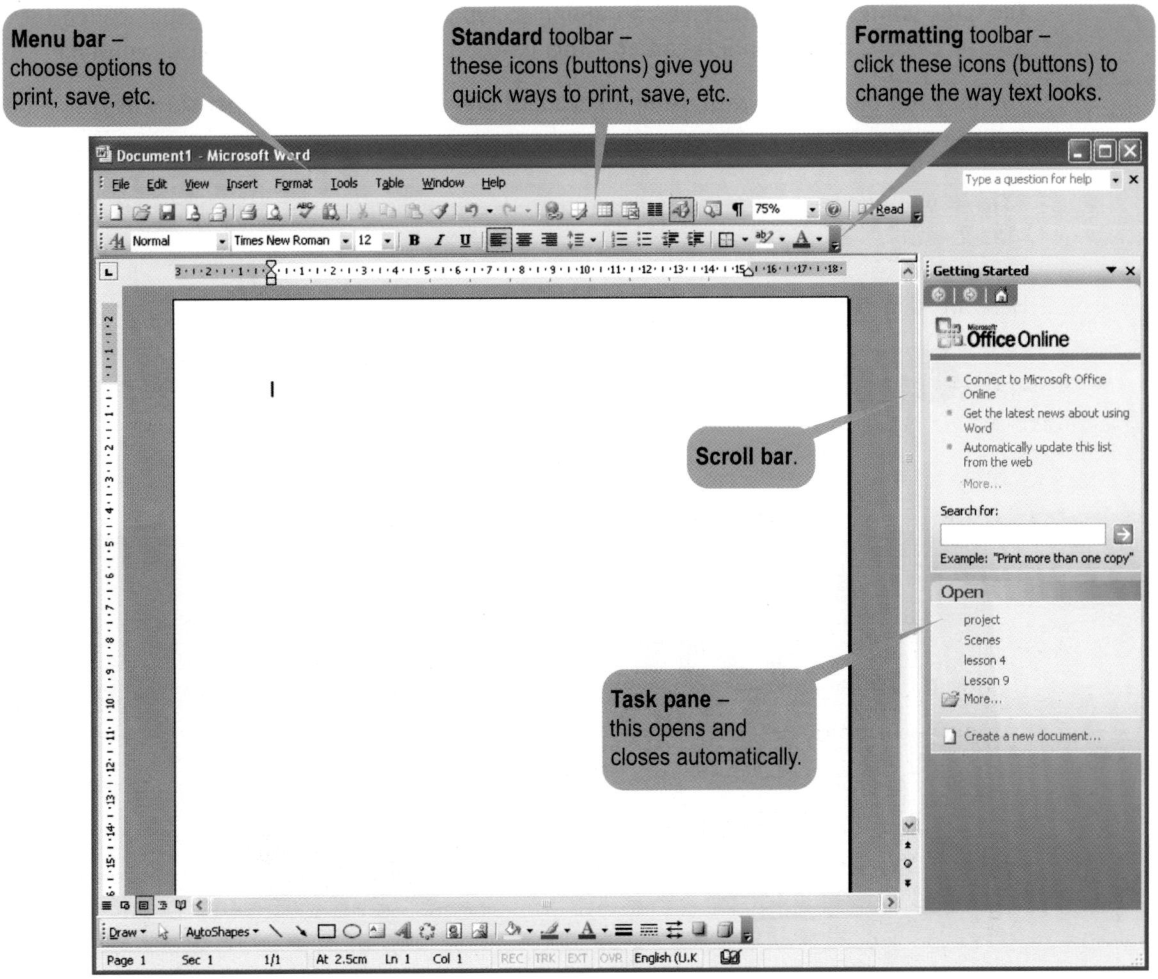

Figure 2.2

This program has a Title bar and a Menu bar (which has nine menus this time). It also has toolbar buttons, which are buttons you can click with the mouse to carry out actions (instead of selecting an option from one of the menu).

The Task pane opens and closes automatically, depending on what you are doing. You can also close the Task pane manually at any time by clicking the Close icon (**X**) in its top right-hand corner.

- Close the Task pane.

Typing practice

The large white area is where you are going to type. You will see a flashing bar, called the insertion point, in the top left corner – this is where the letters will appear as you type.

You may not be familiar with using a keyboard and you will find it rather slow at first – but it's surprising how fast you can get with two fingers!

Tip: If you want to learn how to touch-type, there are plenty of books and CDs available to teach you.

Here are some of the keys you will need to use.

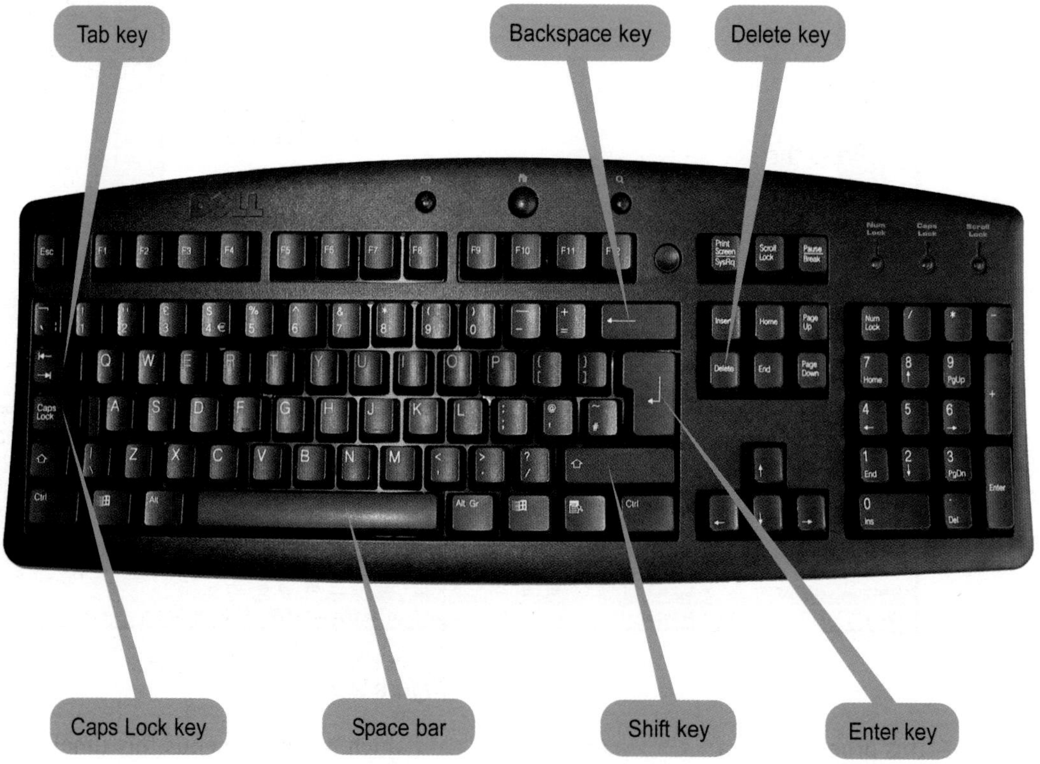

Figure 2.3: A standard keyboard

- Press each of the top row of letter keys:

qwertyuiop

Tip: Word will automatically capitalise the first letter. You will also see a red wavy line because it thinks it is a misspelt word – just ignore this.

- Press the Enter key to move to a new line.
- Press the Caps Lock key and then type the same sequence of keys again. The letters should all appear as capitals:

QWERTYUIOP

Tip: The **Caps Lock** key is called a toggle key – if you press it a second time it goes back to lower-case characters.

- Press the Enter key to move to a new line.
- Press the Caps Lock key to turn it off.
- Press each of the numbered keys on the top row:

1234567890

Tip: If you type the wrong letter, press the **Backspace** key to rub it out.

- Press the Enter key to move to a new line.
- Press the numbered keys again, but this time keep one of the Shift keys held down:

!"£$%^&*( )

Tip: If you press **Enter** in the middle of a line by mistake, some of your text will move to the next line. Press the **Backspace** key to delete the **Enter** character.

This time the symbols above the numbers are displayed. So, holding down the Shift key while you press another key will display either the symbol at the top of the key, or a capital letter (like the Caps Lock key did).

Your screen should now look something like this:

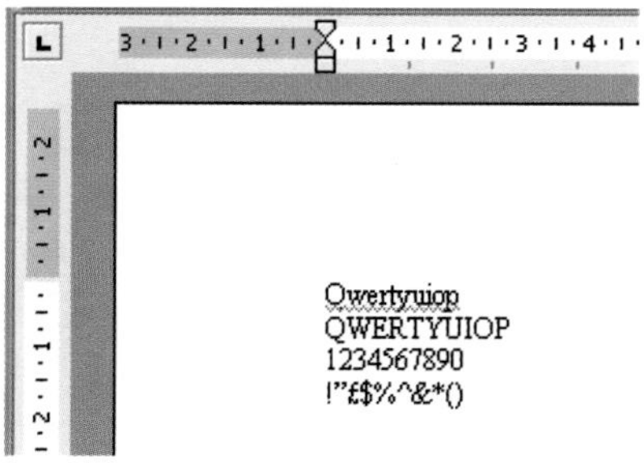

Figure 2.4

The insertion point will be flashing after the last letter you typed. If you move the mouse around, the pointer moves around the screen. The pointer looks different depending on where it is.

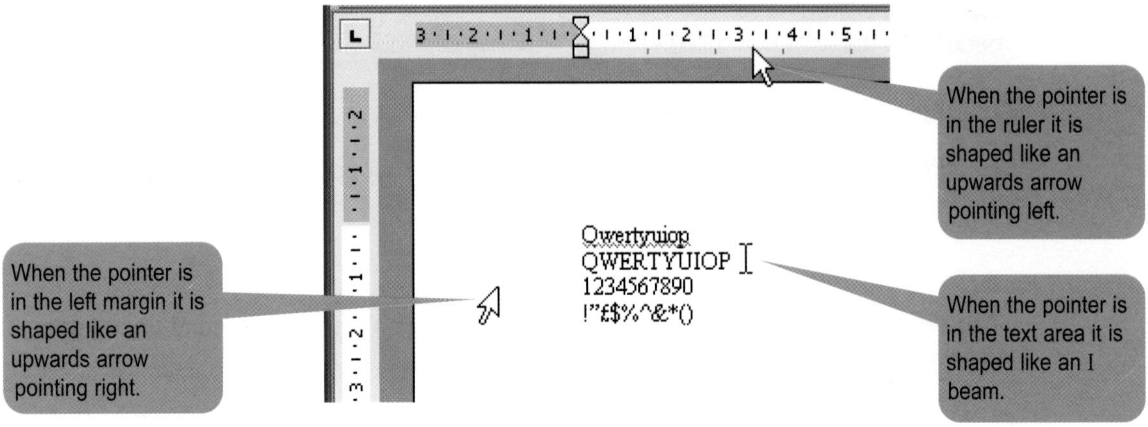
When the pointer is in the ruler it is shaped like an upwards arrow pointing left.
Qwertyuiop
QWERTYUIOP
1234567890
!"£$%^&*()
When the pointer is in the left margin it is shaped like an upwards arrow pointing right.
When the pointer is in the text area it is shaped like an I beam.

Figure 2.5

- Try clicking with the left mouse button in the middle of the text. The insertion point will move to where you clicked and, if you start typing, the letters will appear at that point.

Warning: If you type some new letters and they overwrite the existing text then you are in **overwrite** mode; try pressing the **Insert** key on the keyboard to return you to **insert** mode.

Deleting text

- Practise using the Backspace key to delete characters before the insertion point, and using the Delete key to delete characters after the insertion point.

You could delete all of the text you have typed so far using these two keys, but here's a quicker way.

- Position the pointer in the left margin next to one of the lines of text.
- Click the left mouse button. The line of text next to the pointer should look highlighted: white text on a black background. We call this selected text.
- Press the Delete key and the selected text should disappear.
- Repeat this for each line of text. You should now have a blank screen.
- Practise typing the following sentences, pressing the Space bar to create a space between words. When you reach the end of a line, Word will automatically start a new one for you. You need to press the Enter key only when you want to force a new line.

Juliet and Kirk were quite vexed to be leaving Zanzibar.

We suggest you visit our headquarters in New York whenever you find the time.

The role of the salesman is to negotiate the maximum price.

The amazing vegetables grown by Joyce Thornton quickly earned her the top seven awards at a Produce Show in Essex.

Items Z1879, V5018 and R1428 were missing from the catalogue.

Practise deleting individual characters using the Backspace and Delete keys, and deleting complete rows by selecting them and pressing Delete, by making the following changes:

- Change the name Juliet to Julie.
- In the second sentence, replace the words find the time with can.
- Delete the third sentence completely.
- In the fourth sentence, change the name Joyce to Jayne.
- In the fifth sentence, insert the word new before catalogue.
- Delete everything on the screen.

Typing the letter

- Click at the top-left of the page.
- Practise typing in the following letter. When you reach the end of a line, Word will automatically start a new one for you; but remember to press the Enter key whenever you want to force a new line.

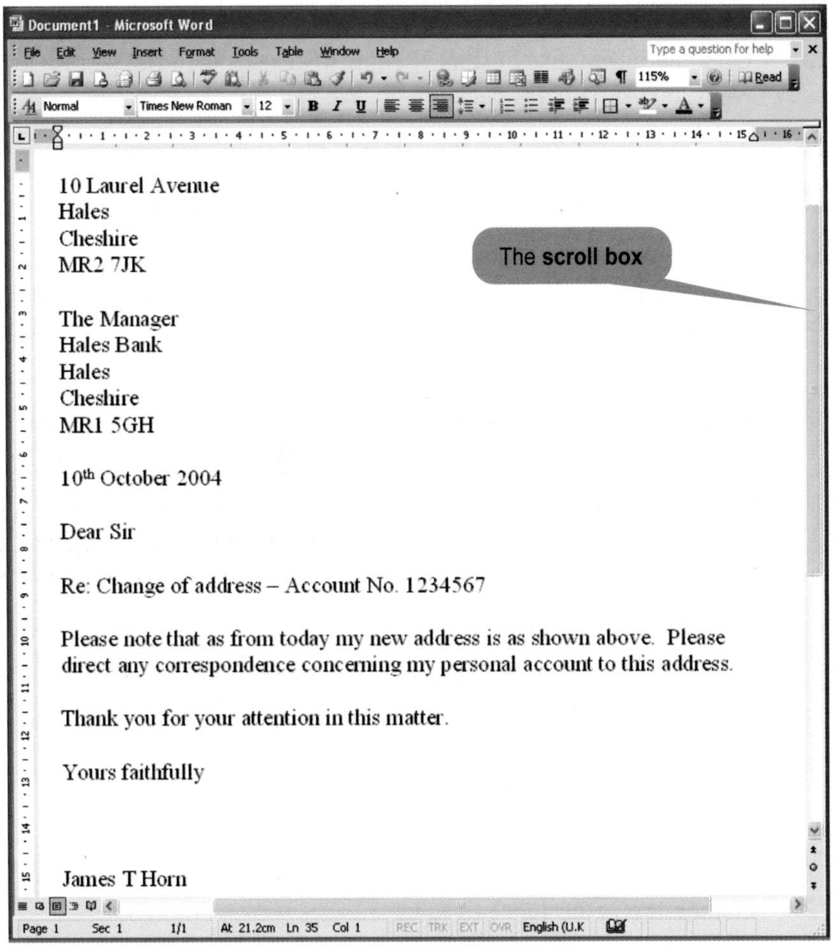
Document1 - Microsoft Word
File Edit View Insert Format Tools Table Window Help
Type a question for help
Normal
Times New Roman
12
115%
Read
10 Laurel Avenue
Hales
Cheshire
MR2 7JK
The Manager
Hales Bank
Hales
Cheshire
MR1 5GH
10th October 2004
Dear Sir
Re: Change of address – Account No. 1234567
Please note that as from today my new address is as shown above. Please direct any correspondence concerning my personal account to this address.
Thank you for your attention in this matter.
Yours faithfully
James T Horn
The scroll box
Page 1 Sec 1 1/1 At 21.2cm Ln 35 Col 1 REC TRK EXT OVR English (U.K

Figure 2.6

Tip: If your screen suddenly goes blank, it may be because you have accidentally scrolled down the page. Try dragging the scroll box back up to the top of the scroll bar. If your mouse has a scroll wheel you can use it to move back to the top of the document.

- Check your letter on the screen and correct any mistakes using the techniques you have just been practising.

Now move on to the next chapter to save all that hard work!

Reminder: There's always the **Help** menu if you get really stuck.

3 Saving

After you have created your letter you will probably want to save it. This will allow you to open it again later, to make changes or to print it out.

All the documents you create on your PC are referred to as files. These files have to be given names; these can be quite long (up to 255 characters) so it is a good idea to use meaningful file names that you can easily find.

As you use your computer more and more you will have lots of files stored on your hard drive. It is extremely important to keep your work organised so that you can go to it quickly.

Files are organised into folders, which are also given names. Folders can also contain other folders (subfolders). One very important folder, which is set up automatically for you, is My Documents. This is where Windows expects you to create your own subfolders to store your work. For example:

Tip: You will see the **My Documents** icon on the desktop

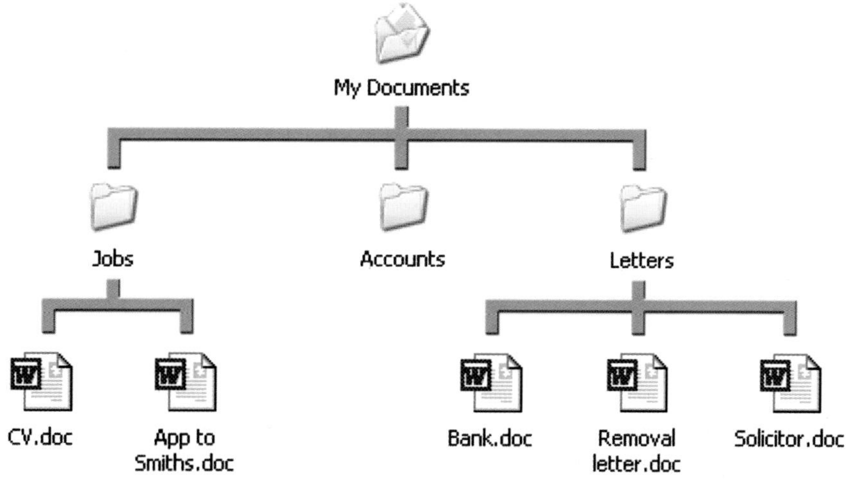

Creating a new folder

So, before you save your work, let's set up a new folder to store it in:

- Do not close Word – leave it open on the screen.
- Click the Start button to display the Start menu.

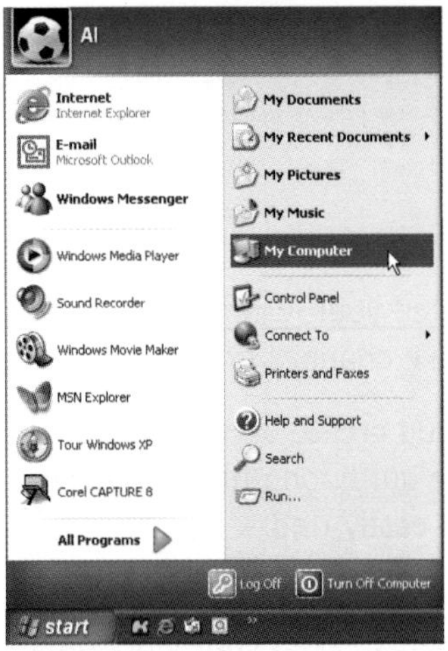

Figure 3.1: Starting My Computer

Tip: You will have different programs from those shown here.

- Click on My Computer.

Tip: If you can't see the blue area of the screen, select **Tools**, **Folder Options** and click on **Restore Defaults**.

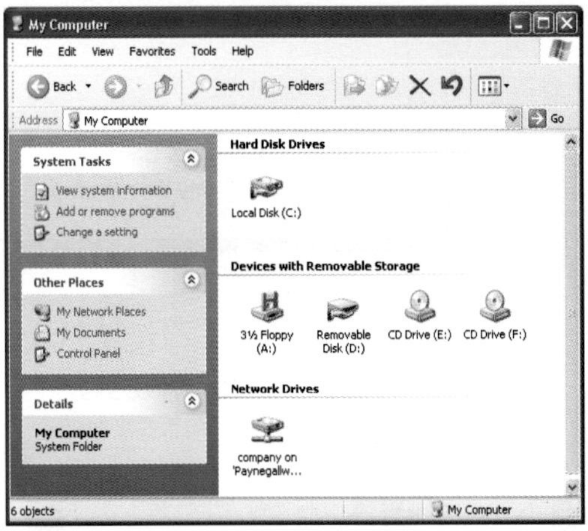

Figure 3.2

Tip: The **A:** drive is normally a floppy disk drive.The **C:** drive is normally the hard disk drive. The **D:** drive is often a CD drive.

- Click on My Documents in the Other Places section.

Note: Some folders may already have been set up for you.

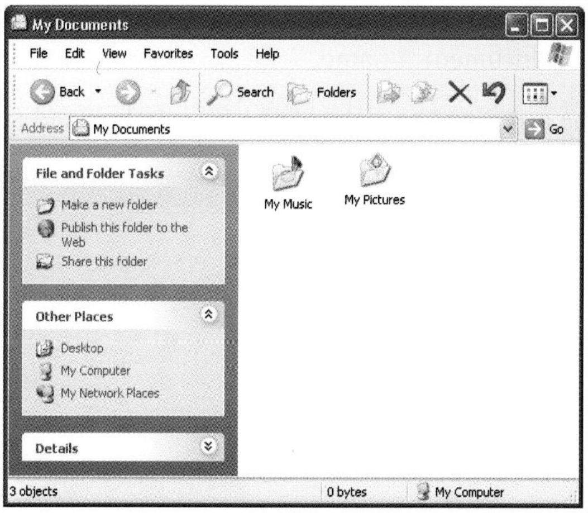

Figure 3.3

Tip: If the contents are displayed differently, click the arrow next to the **Views** button (the last button in the toolbar) and select **Icons**.

The folders that you currently have within My Documents will be displayed on the right.

- Click on Make a new folder in the File and Folder Tasks section.
- In the text box that appears below the new folder icon, type in the name Letters.

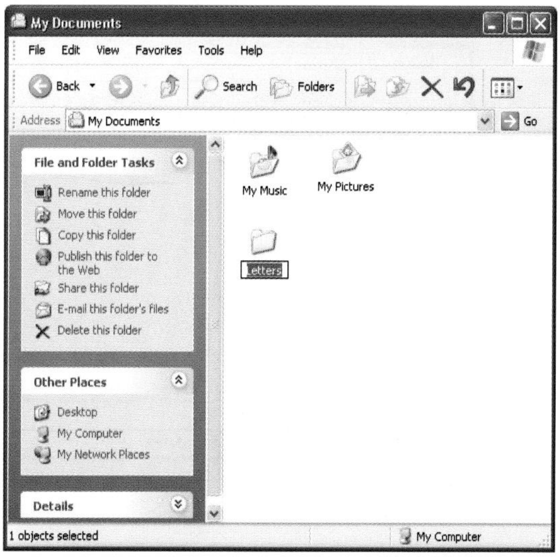

Figure 3.4: Naming the new folder

- Press Enter and close My Computer by clicking the Close Window icon in the top right-hand corner of the window.

Word should still be on your screen with your letter displayed. You can now save the letter in your new folder.

- Select File, Save As. The Save As box will appear. Now you need to find your folder and give your document a name.
- Click the arrow to the right of the Save in box and select My Documents.

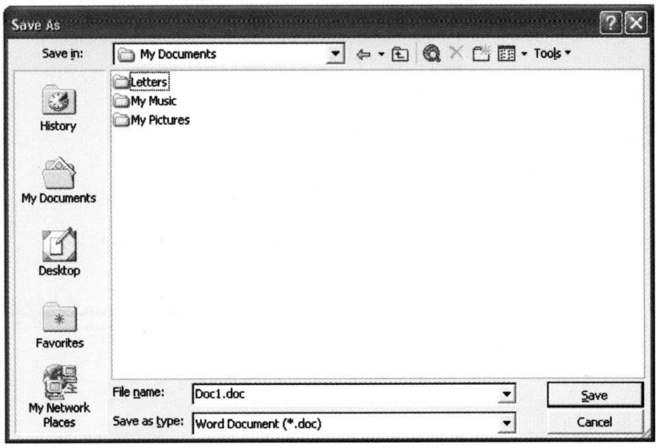

Figure 3.5

- Double-click the Letters folder.

The Save in box changes to Letters, ready for you to save your work into it.

- Double-click at the beginning of the box labelled File name and type a title for your letter; in this case, call it Removal letter.

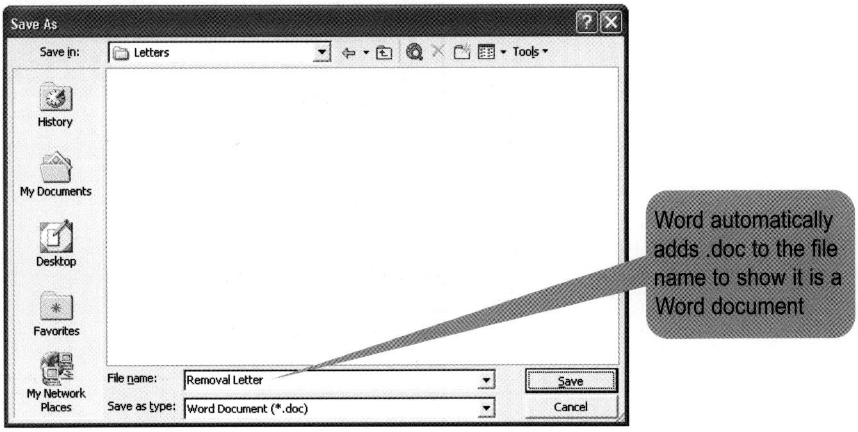

Figure 3.6: Saving the letter

- Click Save.

The Save As box will disappear and your work will be saved. Look at the title bar above your letter the name should have appeared there.

- Close Word by clicking the Close icon.

Tip: Your letter will disappear from the screen – it has been saved on your disk drive.

Copying, moving and deleting files and folders

You can use My Computer to copy, move and delete your files and folders. We will practise copying the file Removal Letter.doc into another new folder and then deleting the original.

Tip: It is recommended that beginners use this procedure to move files. Make a copy first and delete the original only when you are sure it has copied successfully.

- Open My Computer and click on My Documents.
- Click on Make a new folder and name it OurMove.
- Double-click the Letters folder and click the file Removal Letter.doc.

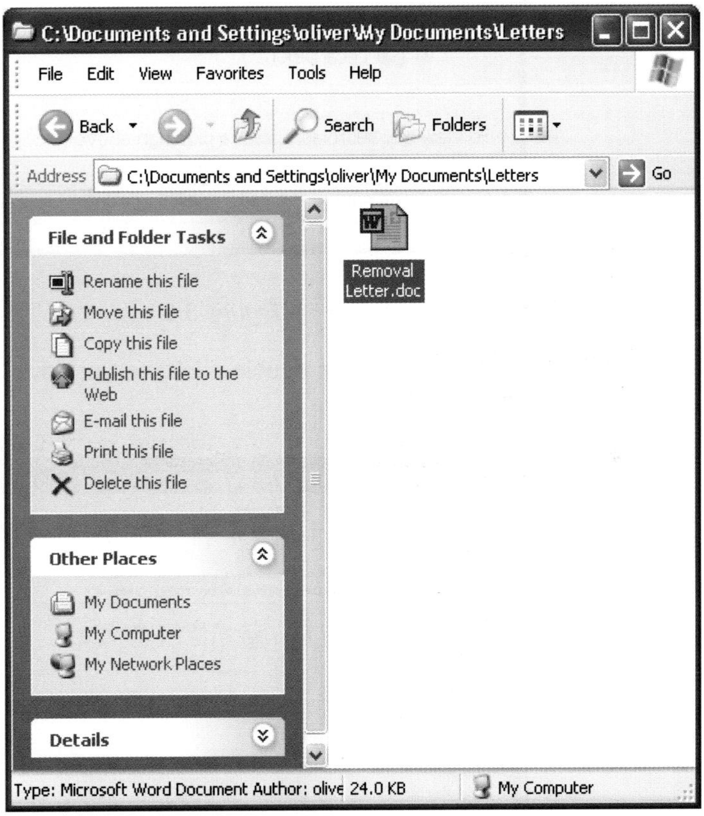

Figure 3.7

Tip: If the file name does not end with **.doc** then you are probably hiding file extensions. It is a good idea to show the file extensions, as follows: open **My Computer**; from the menu, select **Tools**, **Folder Options**; click on the **View** tab; untick the box **Hide file extensions for known file types**; and finally, press **OK**.

- Click Copy this file.

- In the Copy Items window that appears, click on the OurMove folder and then click Copy.

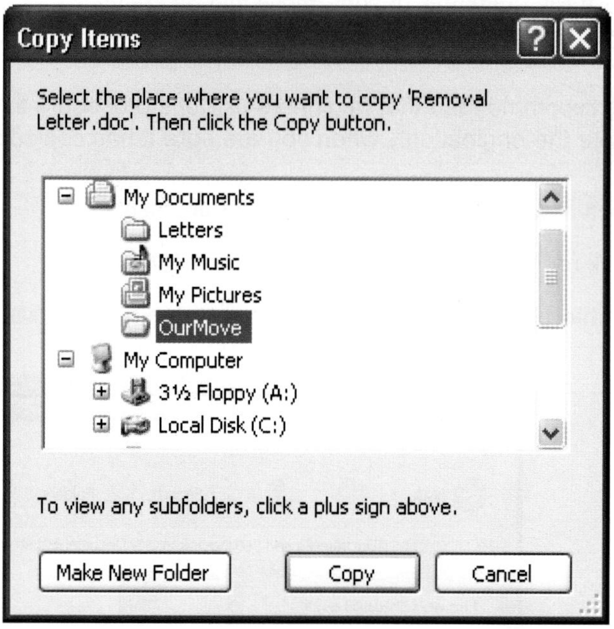

Figure 3.8

- Click on My Documents and then double-click the OurMove folder. You should see a copy of the letter stored in this folder.

Figure 3.9

Now we'll delete the original version of the letter from the Letters folder.

- Click on the Back arrow to return to My Documents.
- Double-click on Letters.
- Click on Removal Letter.doc and then click on Delete this file.

Figure 3.10

- A warning message will appear asking if you are sure you want to delete the file.
- Click Yes to confirm the delete.

The Letters folder should now be empty.

- Close My Computer by clicking the Close Window icon.

Searching for files

If you lose a file you can use the Search facility in My Computer to find it again. We will ask My Computer to find the letter for us again.

- Open My Computer and click the Search button.

Figure 3.11

- In the box on the left, click on Documents.

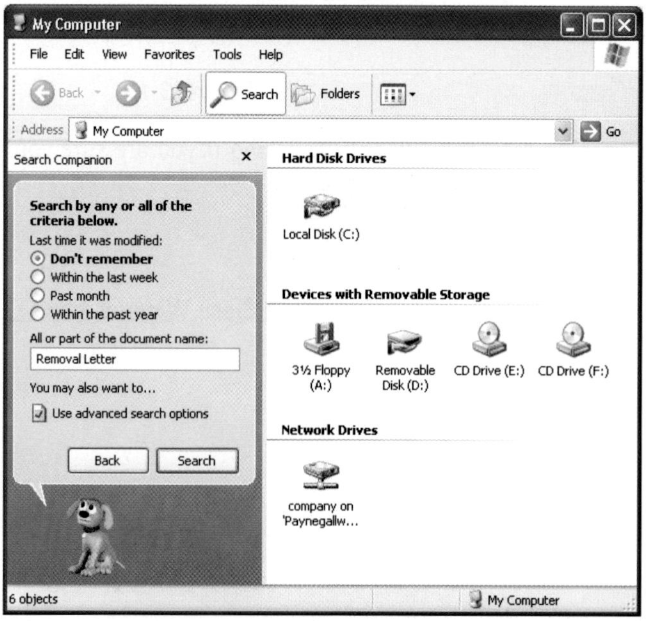

Figure 3.12: Searching for a file

- Type in the name of the file we are looking for (Removal Letter) and click Search.

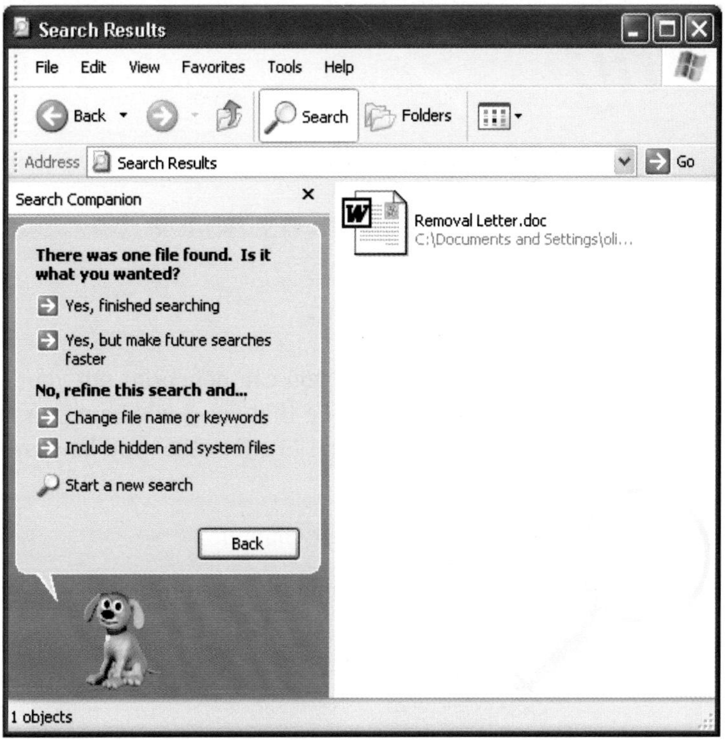

Figure 3.13: The search results

It has found the file we were looking for.

- Click on Removal Letter and details of the file will be displayed in the status bar at the bottom of the window.
- Double-click Removal Letter and the file will open.
- Close the letter and Word by clicking the Close icon.

Printing

4

If you have a printer connected to your PC you can now print out your letter on paper. There are different types of printer but the chances are that yours will be either an ink-jet printer or a laser printer. Refer to the instruction manual to check that you have switched it on and loaded some A4 paper correctly.

Now re-open the letter you saved in the last chapter.

- Open Word as you did at the beginning of Chapter 2.
- Select File, Open.

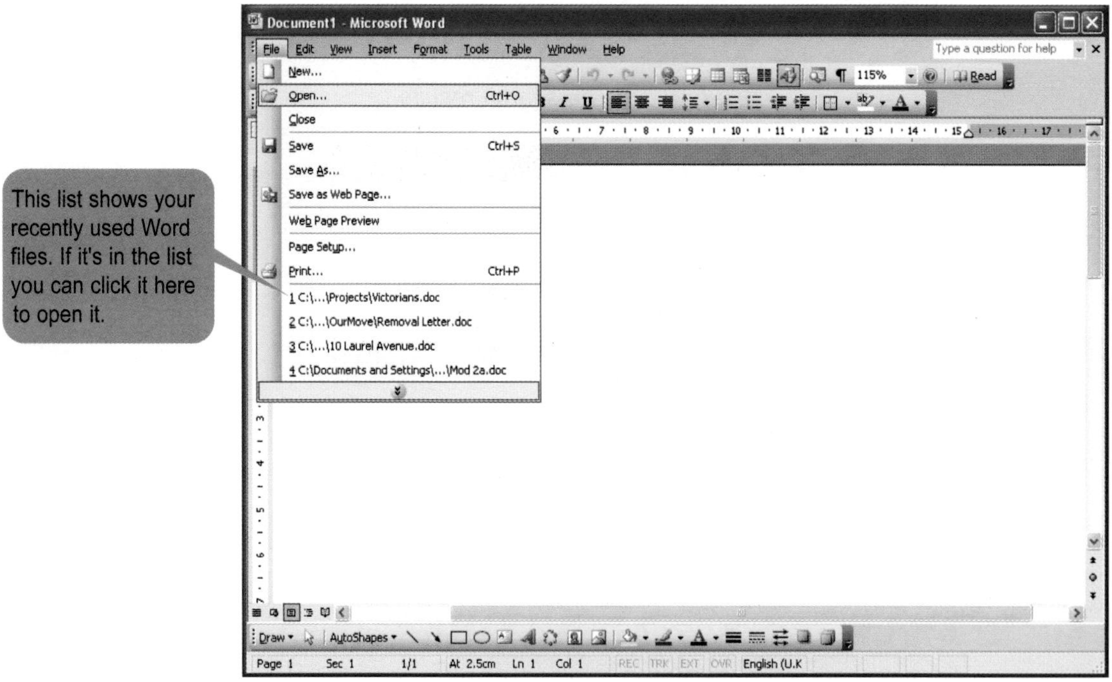

Figure 4.1: Opening a document

- In the Open dialogue box, click on the arrow next to the Look in box and navigate to the Our Move folder. Click on Removal Letter.doc and click Open.

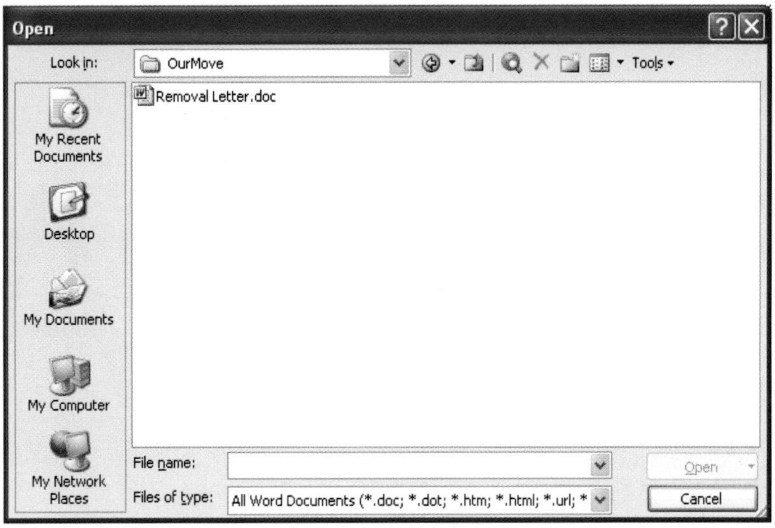

Figure 4.2

Your letter should appear on the screen.

Before you print it there are a few settings that you need to check.

- Select File, Page Setup.

Tip: If you can't see **Page Setup** on the **File** menu, click the small arrow at the bottom to display more options.

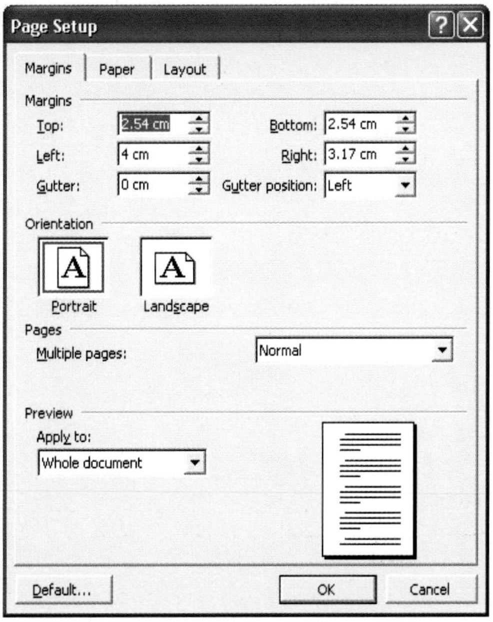

Figure 4.3

This box allows you to change the size and orientation of the paper you will be printing on.

Normally you would print a letter in Portrait orientation.

Portrait

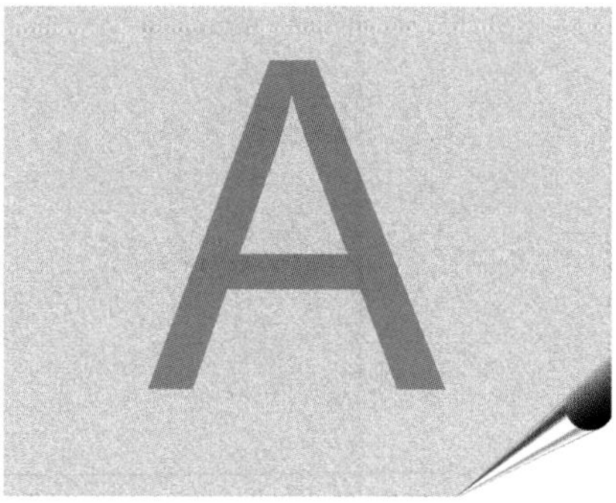

Landscape

Figure 4.4

- Click the Margins tab.
- Make sure the Portrait orientation option is selected.
- Click OK.
- Click the Paper tab.
- If the size is not set to A4, click the down arrow and select A4 from the list.

Print Preview

You must remember that what you see on the screen is not the whole piece of paper. To see how your letter will fit on a sheet of A4 paper you need to use a feature called Print Preview. It is a good idea to use this before printing anything – it can save a lot of paper.

- Click the Print Preview button on the toolbar.

Your letter appears on the image of a piece of A4 paper.

Tip: In **Print Preview**, your mouse pointer changes to a magnifying glass. Click the mouse to zoom in, and click again to zoom out.

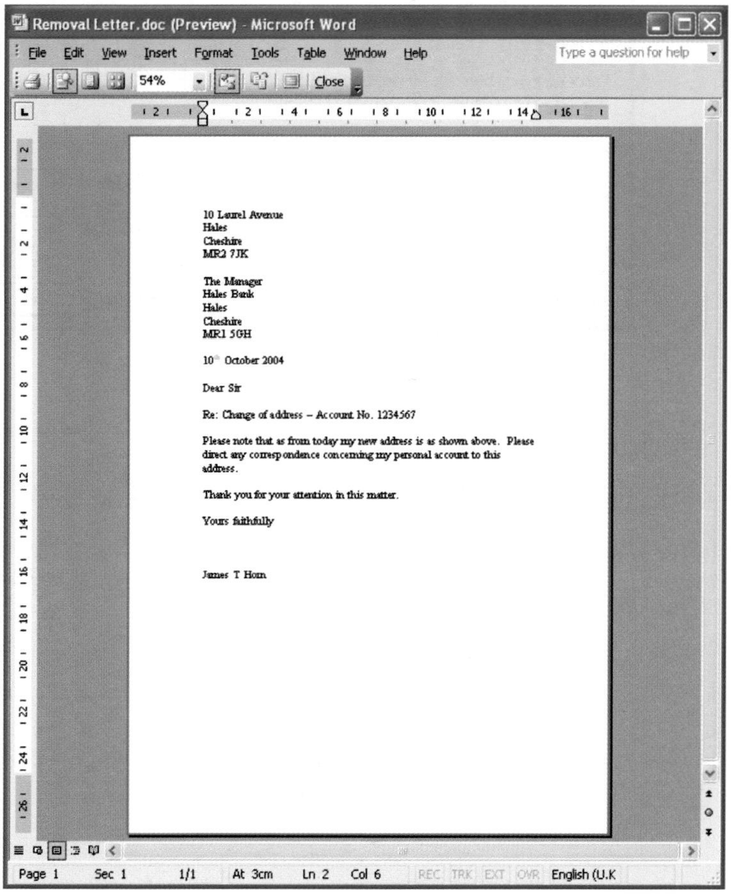

Removal Letter.doc (Preview) - Microsoft Word
File Edit View Insert Format Tools Table Window Help
Type a question for help
54%
Close
10 Laurel Avenue
Hales
Cheshire
MR2 7JK
The Manager
Hales Bank
Hales
Cheshire
MR1 5GH
10th October 2004
Dear Sir
Re: Change of address – Account No. 1234567
Please note that as from today my new address is as shown above. Please direct any correspondence concerning my personal account to this address.
Thank you for your attention in this matter.
Yours faithfully
James T Horn
Page 1 Sec 1 1/1 At 3cm Ln 2 Col 6 REC TRK EXT OVR English (U.K

Figure 4.5: Previewing the letter

If you want to change anything about your letter, now is the time.

- Click Close and you will return to the letter in Word. Make any changes you wish.

- Click the Save button on the toolbar.

- Click the Print Preview button and check your work again.
- If it looks OK, select File, Print.

The dialogue box that appears allows you to choose which printer you want to print to (if you are working on a network), which pages you want to print (for longer documents) and how many copies you would like.

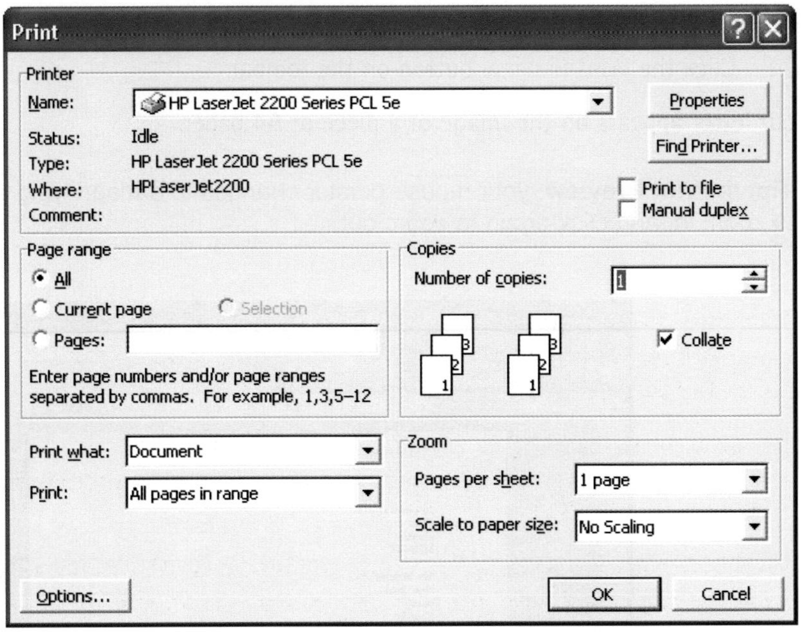

Figure 4.6

- Check that there is some paper in the printer.
- Make sure that Number of copies is set to 1 and click the OK button.

Your letter will print out.

- Close the document by selecting File, Close.

Making a Poster

5

Sometimes the documents you produce need to be eye-catching. Perhaps you need posters to advertise the local village fete or a meeting of the local residents' association, or you might want to advertise something for sale.

Whatever it is, you need to use more of the features available with your word processing package to create different sizes, styles and colours of text, together with colourful pictures to attract people's attention.

In this example we will create an advertisement to display in the window of your car to show that it is for sale. The completed poster should look something like this:

For Sale

LX Vere Saloon

£3995 o.n.o

1979 V Registration

100,000 miles – excellent condition

1 careful lady owner

Telephone 0123 34567 (after 6.00pm)

Figure 5.1: The completed poster

Starting the advertisement

This time it would be better to print the advertisement on landscape paper, so that it will fit in the car window.

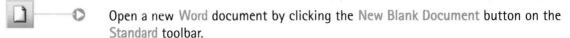

- Open a new Word document by clicking the New Blank Document button on the Standard toolbar.
- Select File, Page Setup and click the Margins tab at the top.
- Click Landscape orientation and then click OK.

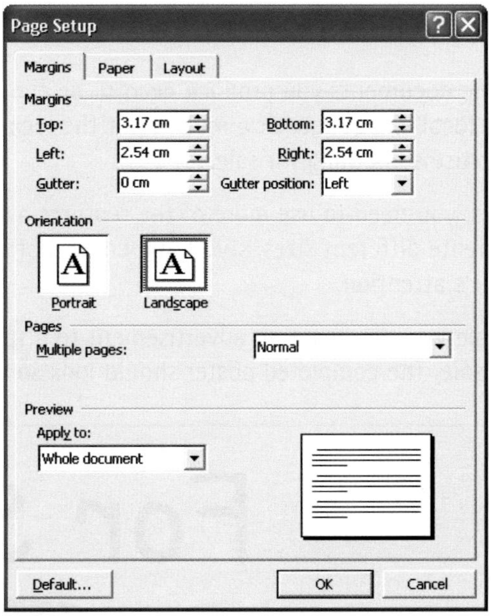

Figure 5.2

When you typed the letter in Chapter 2, all the text was lined up automatically with the left margin – this is called left-aligned text. If you look at the car advertisement, you can see that all the text (except for the telephone number line) is centred on the paper. Text in word processing programs can be left-aligned, centred or right-aligned. You do this by using three buttons on the Formatting toolbar.

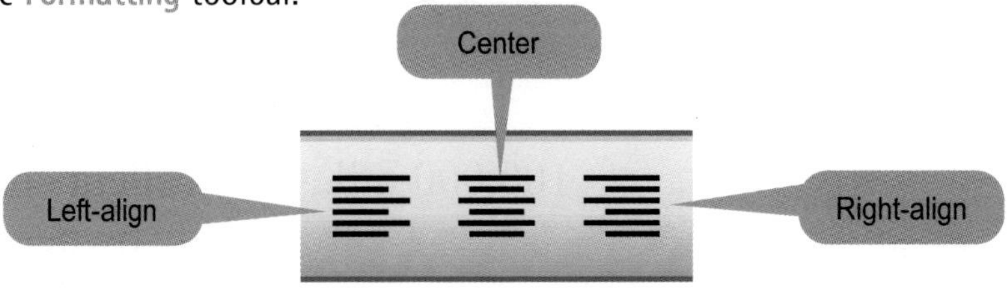

Figure 5.3: Text alignment buttons

- Click the Center button on the Formatting toolbar.

- If the Task pane is open then close it (X).

The insertion point should flash in the middle of the page.

- Type in the words For Sale.

These words need to be much larger so that they will be noticed by passers-by.

- Click the mouse pointer in front of the first letter. Keep the left mouse button pressed down and drag the mouse over the two words. A coloured background appears behind the words – this is called selecting text.

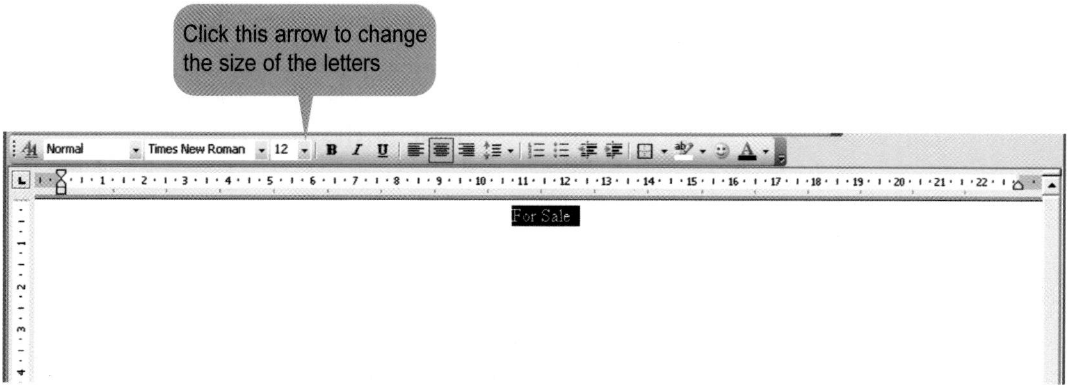
Click this arrow to change the size of the letters
Normal
Times New Roman
12
For Sale

Figure 5.4

Tip: Always use the **Center** button when you need to centre text – never use the **Space bar** to go to the middle of the page.

- Click the arrow shown in Figure 5.4, and from the list that appears click on size 48.

The text should have become much larger.

- Click at the end of the text to deselect it (the black background will disappear).
- Press the Enter key on the keyboard to move to a new line.

Tip: If you want to undo your last action, select **Edit**, **Undo**.

Inserting a picture

Now we will insert a picture of a car. Word comes with a small collection of clip art that you can use in your documents. Clip art is simply a selection of pictures and drawings that have been drawn by professional artists and collected together.

- Select Insert, Picture, Clip Art.

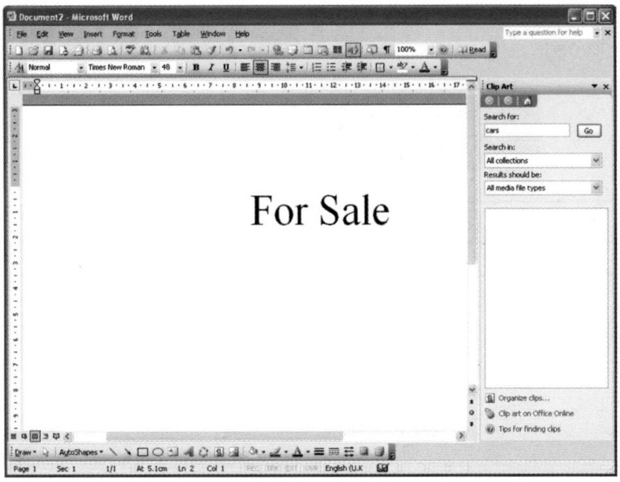

Figure 5.5

- In the Search for box that appears in the Task pane type cars. Click the Go button. A gallery of pictures will appear for you to choose from.
- Click on the picture you want to insert and it will appear in your poster.

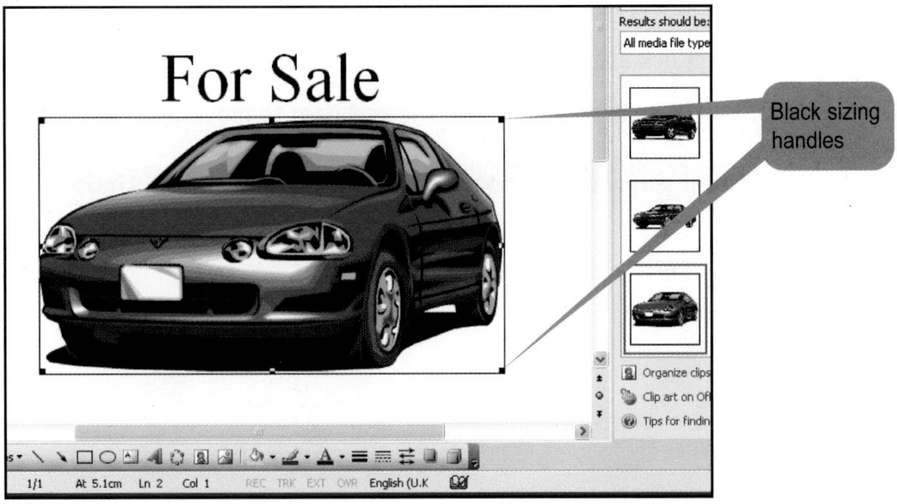

Figure 5.6

Make sure the picture is selected (with the black handles visible). If it is not selected then click it.

You can make the picture bigger or smaller, without changing the proportions, by dragging any of the corner handles.

- Move the mouse pointer over the bottom right handle until it is shaped like a diagonal two-headed arrow.
- Click and hold down the left mouse button.
- Drag downwards and outwards. The car will get bigger.
- Drag upwards and inwards and return the car to its original size.

Note: This is called **sizing** the picture.

- Click next to the car so that the black handles disappear. Press Enter to move to a new line.
- Select File, Save As and save the advert as CarPoster in your My Documents folder.

Completing the text

- The Task pane is open then close it.
- Type in the words LX Vere Saloon.
- Highlight this line of text and change the size to 72.

- While the text is still highlighted, click the Bold button on the Formatting toolbar.

The line of text should now be large and bold.

- Press Enter to move to a new line, and type in the price line £3995 o.n.o.

- Highlight the line and change it to size 26 and bold. This time click the Italic button too.
- Click at the end of the text to deselect it.
- Press Enter and type in the next three lines as shown in Figure 5.1. Make the text size 22, not bold and not italic.

- Move to the next line and click the Left-align button on the Formatting toolbar.
- Press the Tab key on the keyboard, which will move the insertion point a little from the left margin.

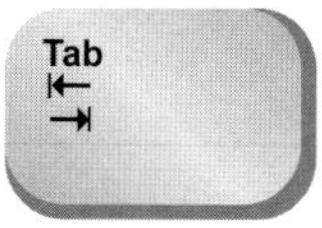

Tip: Tab is next to **Q** on the keyboard.

- Type in the telephone number line in size 18, not bold.

LX Vere Saloon

£3995 o.n.o

1979 V Registration

100,000 miles – excellent condition

1 careful lady owner

Telephone 0123 34567 (after 6.00pm)

Click the Print Preview button on the Standard toolbar to see how the advertisement is coming along.

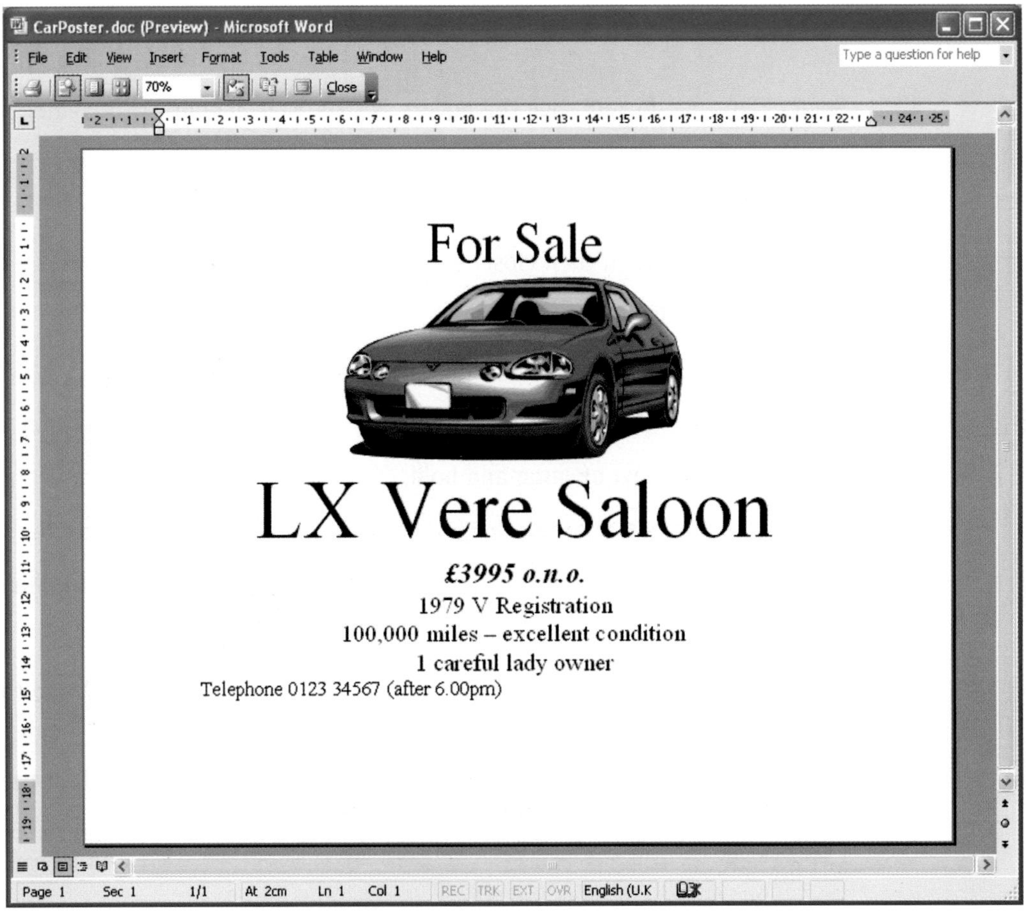

Figure 5.7: A preview of the poster

Remember that you can click the left mouse button to zoom in and magnify the page. Click again to zoom out.

- Click Close to return to the document.

- If you are happy with your work so far then save it again. This time click the Save button on the Standard toolbar.

Changing the page margins

Margins are the white spaces to the top, bottom, left and right of a page. On our advertisement the top and bottom margins seem too deep. We will make them smaller to give us more room on the page.

- Click the Close button on the Print Preview toolbar.
- Select File, Page Setup.
- Enter 2.0 cm for the top and bottom margins and click OK.

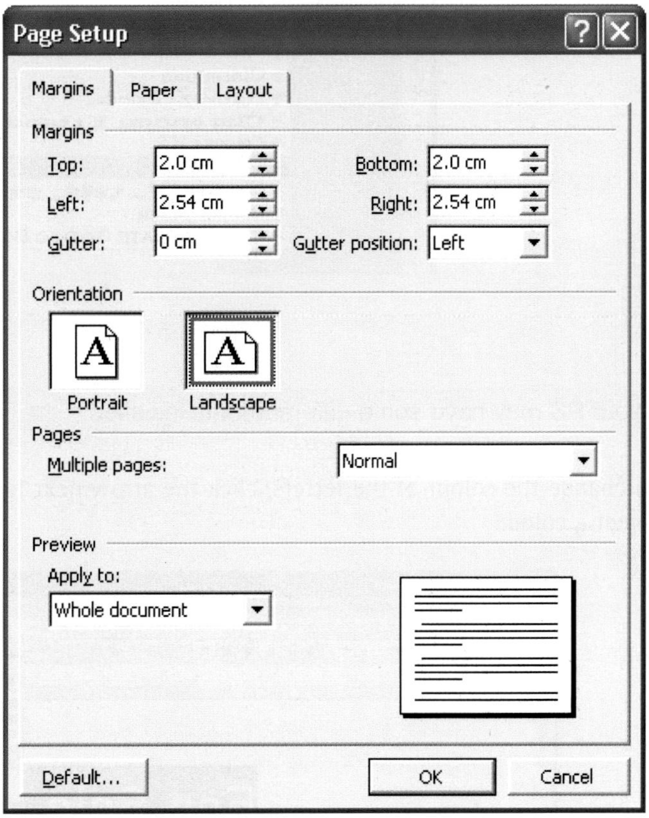

Figure 5.8: Changing margins

If you look at the document in Print Preview again, you will see we have created some extra space at the bottom of the page.

Changing the style of text

In the completed advertisement shown in Figure 5.1, you will see that the first line For Sale is emphasised by being in a different font (style of lettering) and colour.

- Highlight the words For Sale.
- Change the font to Comic Sans MS by clicking on the arrow shown below and scrolling down the list of fonts. Click on Comic Sans MS.

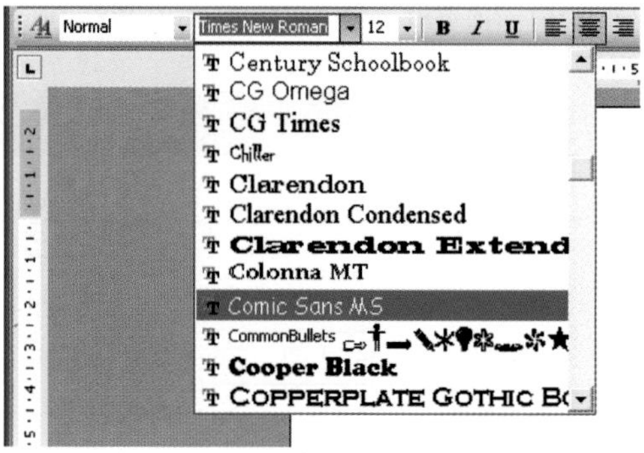

Figure 5.9

Note: Your PC may have some different fonts installed.

- To change the colour of the letters, click the arrow next to the Font Color button and select a colour.

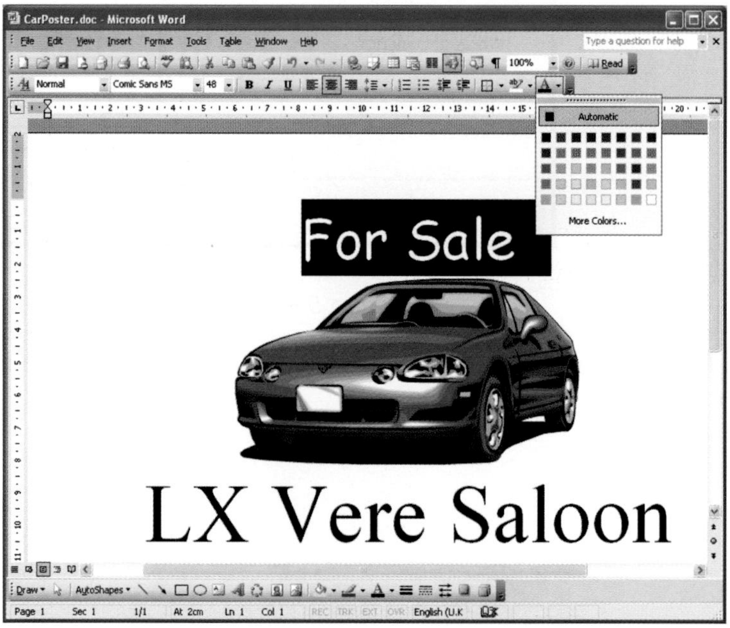

Figure 5.10: Changing the font colour

- Practise changing the size, colour and style of different lines of text. Insert some extra blank lines if you think the poster needs spacing out more.
- Use Print Preview to see how you have improved the document.
- Now save your advertisement and print it out.
- Close Microsoft Word.

For Sale
LX Vere Saloon
£3995 o.n.o
1979 V Registration
100,000 miles – excellent condition
1 careful lady owner
Telephone 0123 34567 (after 6.00pm)

Figure 5.11

Note: If you would like to learn more about **Microsoft Word**, try another book in this series – ***Word 2003 Right from the Start***.

Household Accounts 6

What is a spreadsheet?

Spreadsheets help you to organise numbers and words into neat columns and rows. Some special features allow you to perform calculations on the numbers, sort lists alphabetically or numerically and create graphs and colourful charts from your spreadsheets.

Spreadsheets are used by most businesses working with financial data. They are often used in the home too, for household accounts and planning budgets – for the family holiday perhaps. Different figures can be entered, and the effect of the changes will be calculated automatically.

There are many different spreadsheet packages that you can purchase to run on your PC. This example uses Microsoft Excel 2003.

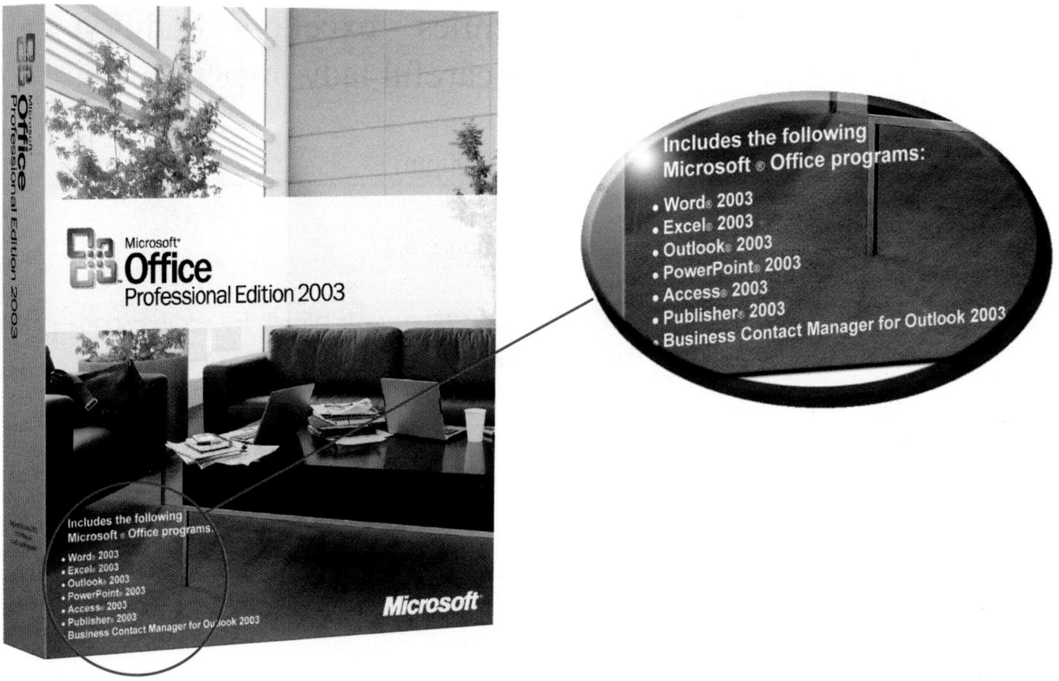

Fact: Microsoft Word and **Microsoft Excel** are supplied as part of **Microsoft Office**.

Getting started

- Load Microsoft Excel by selecting it from the list of programs on the Start menu.

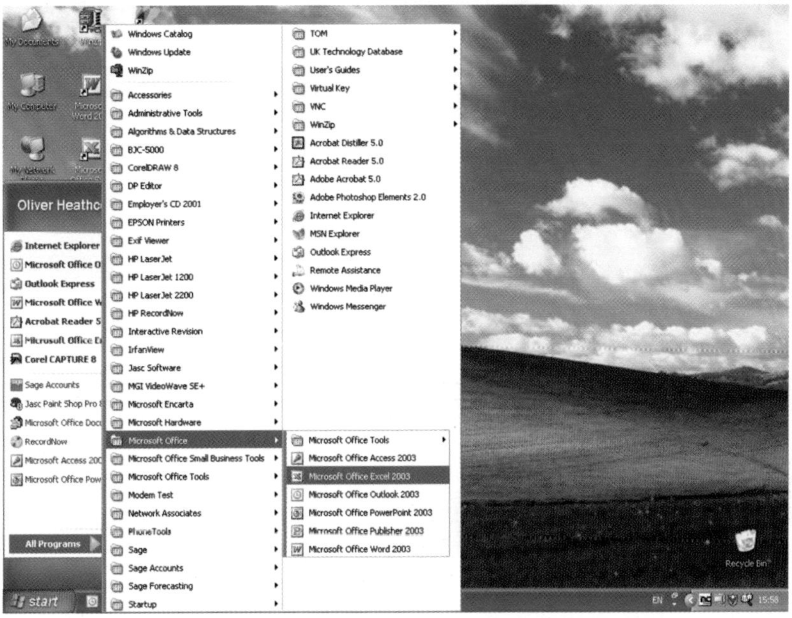

Figure 6.1: Starting Excel

Your screen should look like the one below:

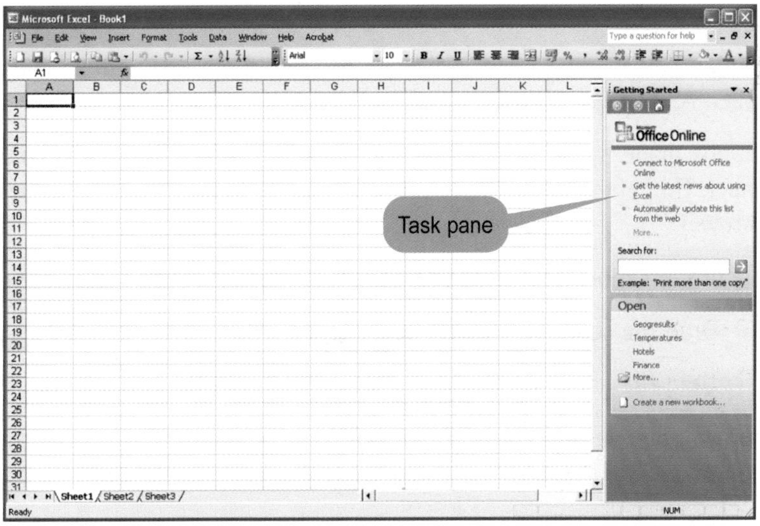

Figure 6.2

- Click on Create a new workbook in the Task pane.
- Click on Blank workbook in the Task pane.

Your screen should now look like this:

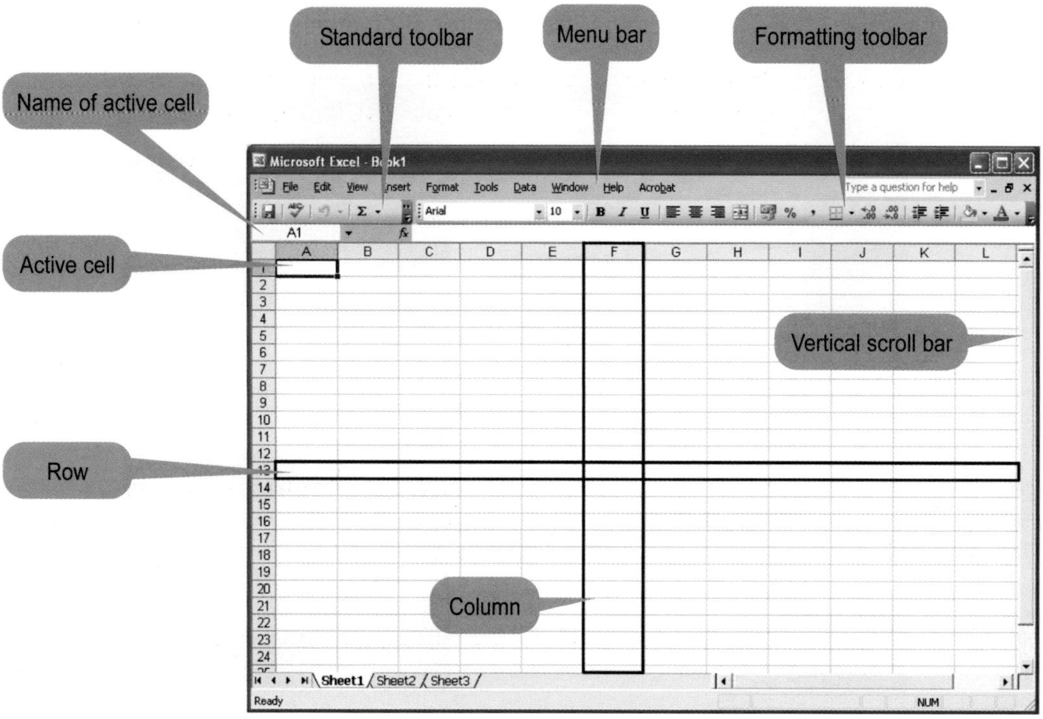

Figure 6.3

On the opening screen you can see a menu bar and toolbar rather like you used when you were word processing.

The main part of the screen is divided into a grid of rows and columns. The columns are labelled A, B, C, etc., and the rows are labelled 1, 2, 3, etc.

Each box made by the grid is called a cell and is referred to by its column letter and row number. The reference of the cell in the top left-hand corner is A1, because it is in column A and row 1.

There are lots more cells in the spreadsheet that you can't see at the moment.

- Drag the scroll bars to see some of the other empty cells.
- Drag the bars back again so that cell A1 is in the top left-hand corner.

When you open a new spreadsheet, cell A1 is highlighted – we call this the active cell. When you start typing, the letters or numbers will appear in this cell.

There are several different ways to change which cell is active. Try these out:

- Move the pointer using the mouse and click in the cell you want to change.
- Press the Tab key on the keyboard to select the next cell to the right as the active cell.
- Use one of the arrow keys on the keyboard to go up, down, left or right.

Entering text

Let's set up a spreadsheet for the household accounts.

We will record all incomings and outgoings over a six-month period. The spreadsheet will calculate the remaining balance each month and a cumulative balance over the six months.

- If the Task pane on the right of the screen is still open, close it by clicking its Close icon.
- Click in cell A1 to ensure that this is the active cell.
- Type the heading Accounts.
- Now click in cell A3 and type the label Incoming.
- Click in cell B2 and type January.
- Press the right arrow key to move to cell C2, and type February.

Now highlight cells B2 and C2 and drag the small fill handle in the bottom right-hand corner to cell G2. Excel understands that you are listing the months of the year and fills them in automatically for you: we call this Auto Fill.

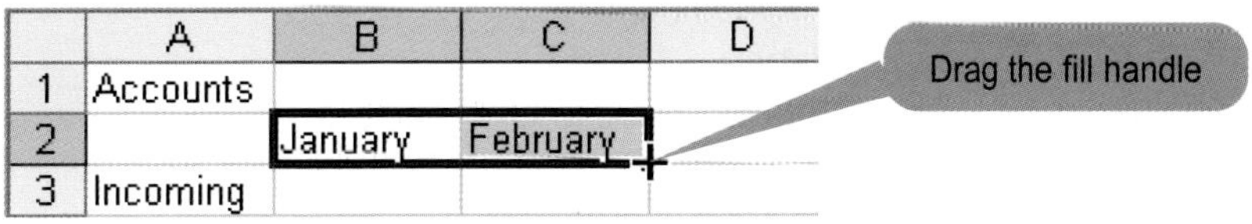

Figure 6.4

- Type the remaining items into cells A3 to A24 as shown in Figure 6.5.

	A	B	C	D	E	F	G
1	Accounts						
2		January	February	March	April	May	June
3	Incoming						
4	Salary						
5	Family allowance						
6	Totals						
7	Outgoing						
8	Mortgage						
9	Council tax						
10	Gas						
11	Electricity						
12	Telephone						
13	TV licence						
14	Satellite TV						
15	Car insurance						
16	Car tax						
17	Food						
18	Clothing						
19	Entertainment						
20	Petrol						
21	Totals						
22							
23	Balance each month						
24	Cumulative balance						

Figure 6.5

Tip: Don't worry about the contents of column **A** spilling over into column **B** – we will fix it later.

Editing data

The heading on the spreadsheet should have been Household Accounts, not Accounts. There are several ways of putting this right, but we will try one of the simplest.

- Click in cell A1, which contains the heading Accounts. You will see that the text also appears in the Formula bar.

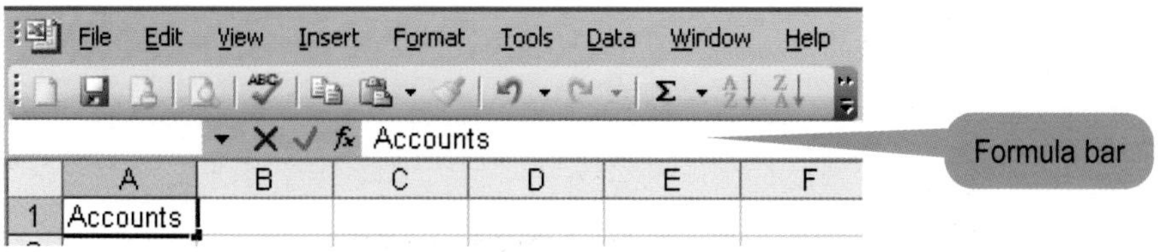

Figure 6.6

Click in the Formula bar before the letter A.

- Type in the word Household, followed by a space. You will notice that the letters appear in cell A1 at the same time.
- Press Enter to register the change.

Deleting data

Suppose we decide that we do not want to include entertainment and petrol in the list of outgoings (cells A19 and A20). We can delete them.

- Click in cell A19, keep your finger down on the left mouse button, and drag down into cell A20 to select the two cells.

Tip: You will notice that when you select spreadsheet cells, the first one in the selection remains white.

Figure 6.7: Selecting cells

- Press the Delete key on the keyboard.

The contents of cells A19 and A20 should have disappeared.

Remember that if you accidentally delete something there is no need to panic. Suppose we decide we *would* like to include entertainment and petrol in our calculations: we now need to undo the deletion.

- Select Edit, Undo Clear, and the text should reappear.

Making columns wider

Let's make column A wider, so that all of the contents fit in without spilling over into column B.

- Move your pointer between the column headers (see Figure 6.10) for columns A and B.
- When the pointer changes to a left- and right-pointing arrow (see Figure 6.8), click and drag to the right.

Figure 6.8: Sizing a column

The spreadsheet should look clearer now.

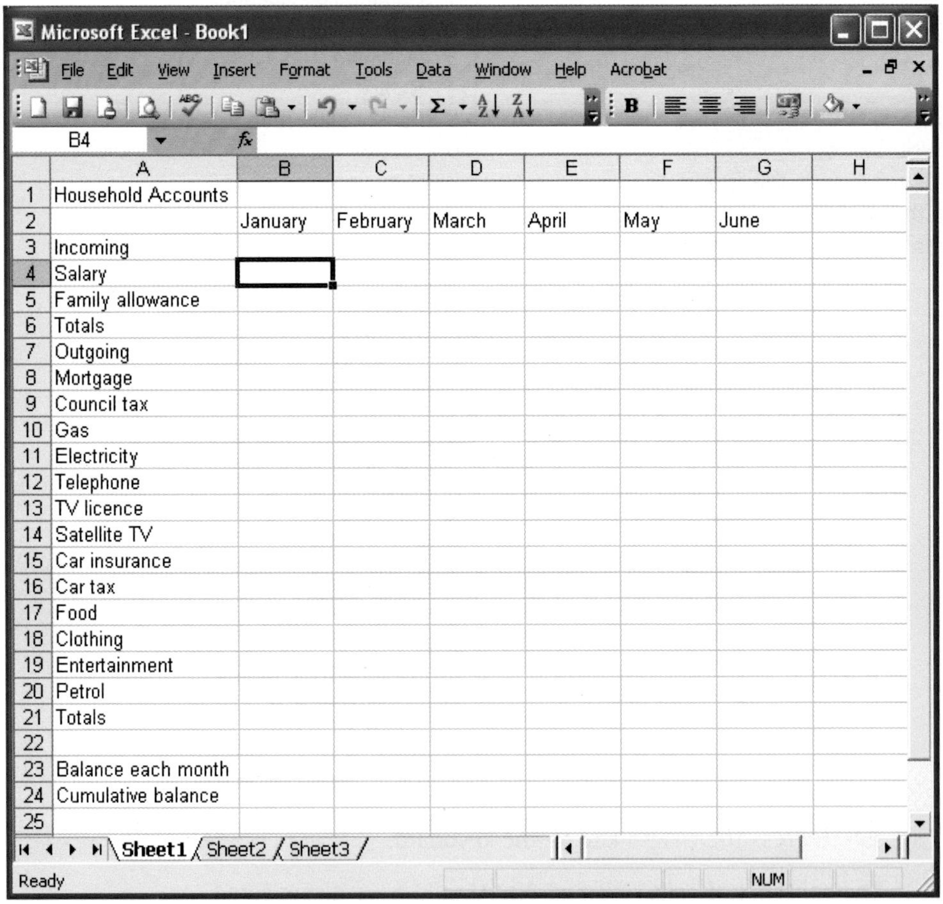

Figure 6.9: The spreadsheet so far

Reminder: Use the **Help** menu or press **F1** for help if you run into problems.

Inserting and deleting rows and columns

We can delete the whole of row 22 so that there is no gap between Totals and Balance each month.

- Right-click the row header for row 22 and select Delete Row from the shortcut menu.

The next line of text moves up to row 22.

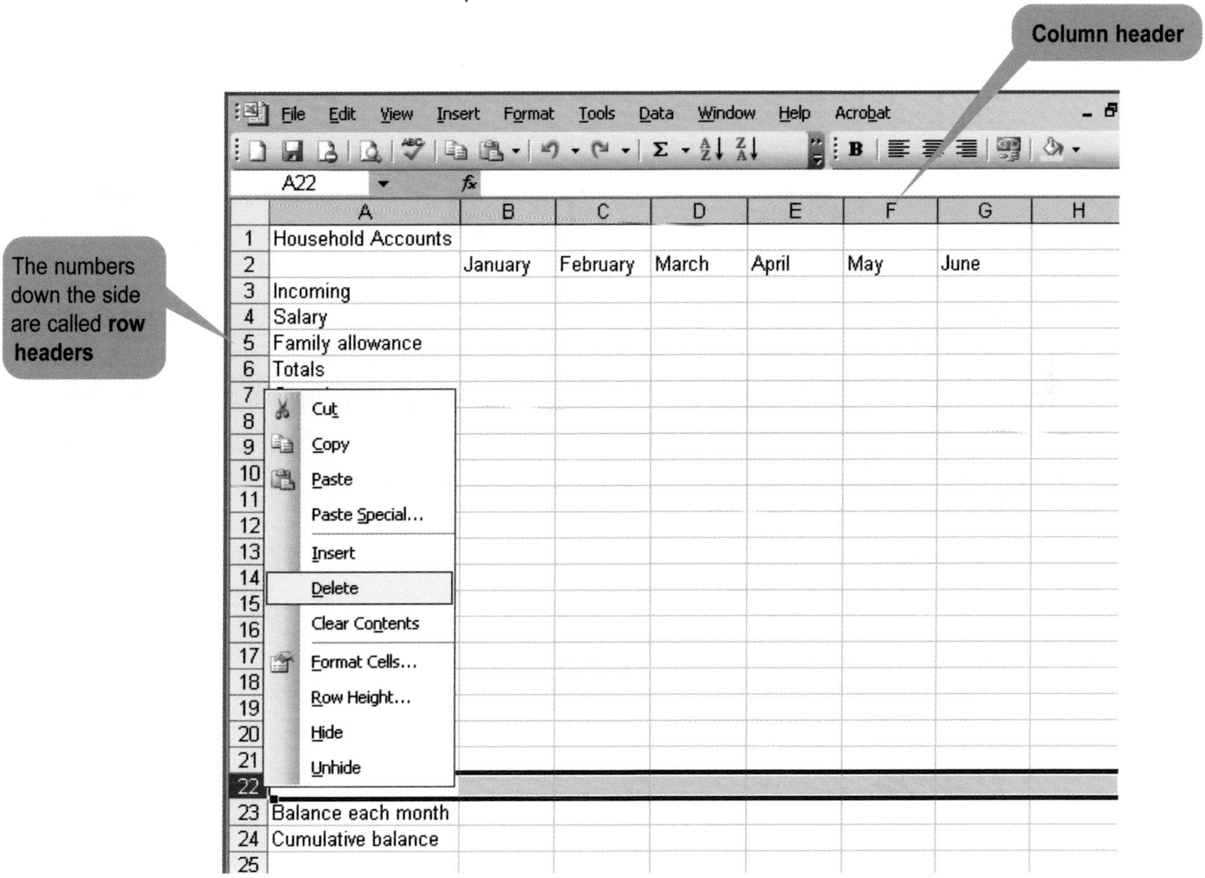

Figure 6.10: Deleting a row

Tip: You can delete columns in the same way.

- Use the Undo button to bring back the blank line.

Inserting rows and columns is also very simple. Let's insert another row in between rows 6 and 7.

- Right-click the row header for row 7 and select Insert from the shortcut menu.

A new row is automatically inserted.

- Insert a new row between rows 21 and 22 and type Holidays in cell A22.

Inserting the data

Now we will enter the data shown in Figure 6.12. When the same entry is repeated in several cells you can use the fill handle to speed up the data entry, for example:

- Click in cell B4, enter the value 1250 and press Enter.
- Click on cell B4 again and drag the fill handle to cell G4 to repeat the value across the row.

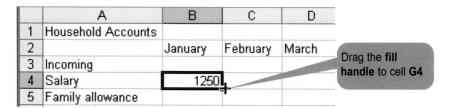

	A	B	C	D
1	Household Accounts			
2		January	February	March
3	Incoming			
4	Salary	1250		
5	Family allowance			

Drag the **fill handle** to cell **G4**

Figure 6.11

Tip: When you copy using **Auto Fill**, you may see a **smart tag**. Just ignore this for the moment.

- Use this technique to enter the rest of the data.

	A	B	C	D	E	F	G	H
1	**Household Accounts**							
2		January	February	March	April	May	June	
3	Incoming							
4	Salary	1250	1250	1250	1250	1250	1250	
5	Family allowance	60	60	60	60	60	60	
6	Totals							
7								
8	Outgoing							
9	Mortgage	300	300	300	300	300	300	
10	Council tax	75	75	75	75	75	75	
11	Gas	30	30	30	30	30	30	
12	Electricity	25	25	25	25	25	25	
13	Telephone			120			120	
14	TV licence	110						
15	Satellite TV	20	20	20	20	20	20	
16	Car insurance		180					
17	Car tax		120					
18	Food	350	350	350	350	350	350	
19	Clothing	50	50	50	50	50	50	
20	Entertainment	100	100	100	100	100	100	
21	Petrol	60	60	60	60	60	60	
22	Holidays					800		
23	Totals							
24								
25	Balance each month							
26	Cumulative balance							
27								

Figure 6.12

Note: Change these to match your incomings and outgoings if you wish.

Saving your work

- Select File, Save As.

A screen will be displayed rather like the one that you used to save your word processing documents.

- Make sure that you are in the correct folder.
- Type in a meaningful filename, for example HouseholdAccounts.
- Click Save.

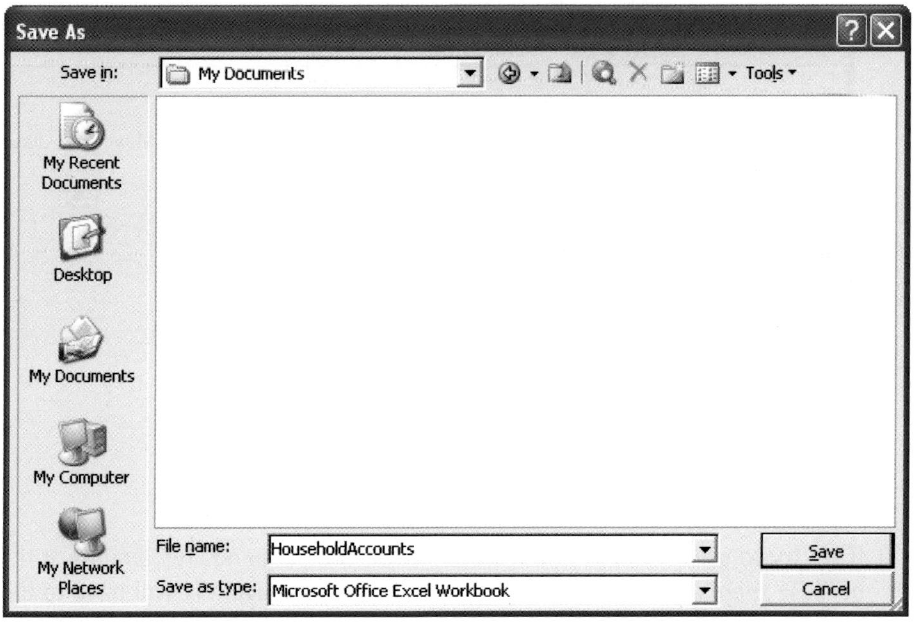

Figure 6.13: Saving the spreadsheet

Using formulae

Now for the fun part – entering some formulae so that Excel will perform the calculations automatically for you.

First we need to calculate monthly totals for incoming and outgoing items.

- Click in cell B6 and click the AutoSum button on the Standard toolbar.

Excel guesses which cells you want to sum. Your screen will look like this:

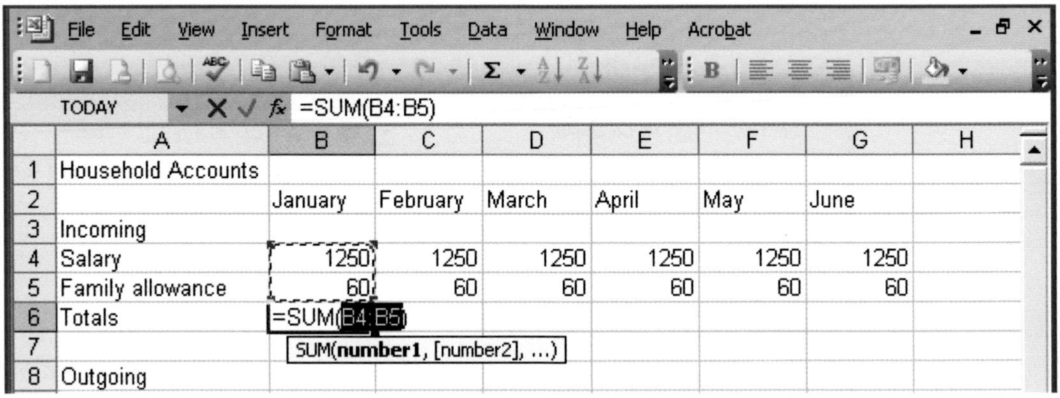

Figure 6.14

- Press Enter. The answer 1310 appears.
- Copy this formula to cells C6 to G6 using the fill handle.

If we try to use AutoSum in cell B23 to total the outgoings for January, it doesn't work; this is because there are some empty cells in the column above. We will have to enter a formula from scratch.

Formulae are entered using cell references and are always preceded by the equals sign (=).

They use the following mathematical symbols:

+	Add
-	Subtract
*	Multiply
/	Divide

We could type =B9+B10+B11 and so on into cell B23, but this would be a very long formula. Instead we can use the SUM function, which AutoSum automatically used (see Figure 6.14).

- Click in cell B23 and type =SUM(B9:B22). This means we want to add up the contents of cells B9 to B22.
- Press Enter. The answer will appear.
- Use the fill handle to copy the formula to cell G23.

In row 25 we want to calculate the balance we have left each month (Incomings minus Outgoings).

- In cell B25 enter the formula =B6-B23 and press Enter.
- Copy this formula across to G25 using the fill handle.

To produce the cumulative balances in row 26 we need to keep adding up the balances from each month.

- In cell B26 enter the formula =B25 and press Enter.
- In cell C26 enter the formula =B26+C25 and press Enter.
- Copy the formula in cell C26 across to cell G26. Have a look at Figure 6.15 – does yours look the same?

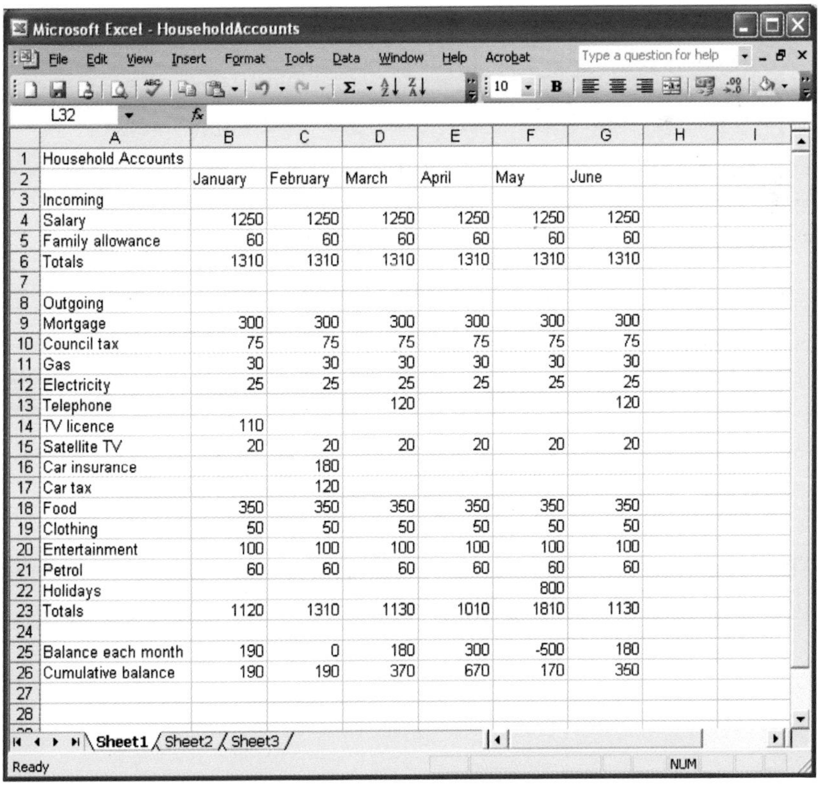

	A	B	C	D	E	F	G
1	Household Accounts						
2		January	February	March	April	May	June
3	Incoming						
4	Salary	1250	1250	1250	1250	1250	1250
5	Family allowance	60	60	60	60	60	60
6	Totals	1310	1310	1310	1310	1310	1310
7							
8	Outgoing						
9	Mortgage	300	300	300	300	300	300
10	Council tax	75	75	75	75	75	75
11	Gas	30	30	30	30	30	30
12	Electricity	25	25	25	25	25	25
13	Telephone			120			120
14	TV licence	110					
15	Satellite TV	20	20	20	20	20	20
16	Car insurance		180				
17	Car tax		120				
18	Food	350	350	350	350	350	350
19	Clothing	50	50	50	50	50	50
20	Entertainment	100	100	100	100	100	100
21	Petrol	60	60	60	60	60	60
22	Holidays					800	
23	Totals	1120	1310	1130	1010	1810	1130
24							
25	Balance each month	190	0	180	300	-500	180
26	Cumulative balance	190	190	370	670	170	350
27							
28							

Figure 6.15

Formatting the spreadsheet

You will see that text by default appears to the left in a spreadsheet cell (left-aligned) and numbers appear to the right (right-aligned). Let's right-align the headings above the currency cells so that they line up, and make the text bold.

The spreadsheet would look better if the months in row 2 were right-aligned like the numbers.

- Select cells B2 to G2 and click the Align Right button on the Standard toolbar.

- While the cells are still selected, click the Bold button.
- Make the labels in cells A1, A3, A6, A8, A23, A25 and A26 bold.

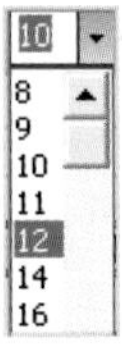

- Change the size of the main heading in cell A1 to 12 by clicking the arrow next to the Font Size button.
- Make cells A6 and A23 right-aligned.

Cells B6 to G6 and cells B23 to G23 need top and bottom borders.

- Highlight cells B6 to G6.

- Click the arrow to the right of the Borders button on the Formatting toolbar.
- Click the Top and Bottom Border option.
- Repeat for cells B23 to G23.

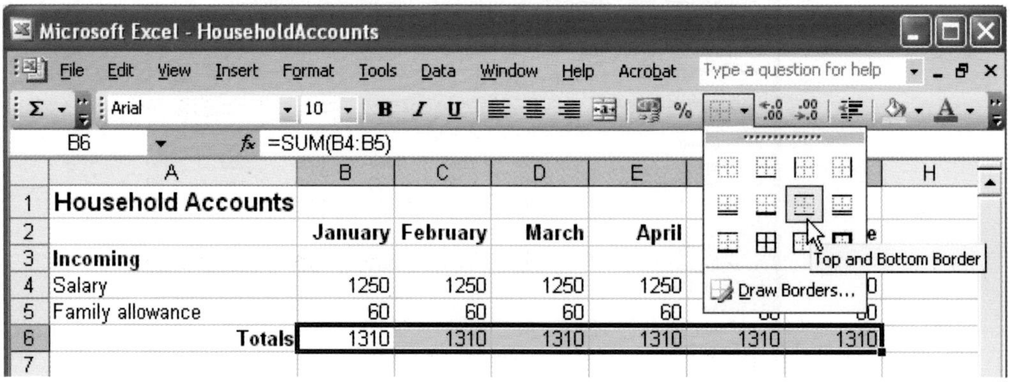

Figure 6.16: Adding borders

Tip: You can select non-adjacent cells by clicking in the first cell and then keeping your finger on the **Ctrl** key as you click the others.

Cell G26 contains the balance remaining after the six-month period. We'll shade this cell to make it stand out.

- Click in cell G26.

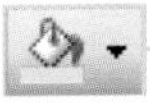

- Click the arrow to the right of the Fill Color button on the Formatting toolbar and choose a colour.

- If the number is now difficult to see then use the Font Color button on the Formatting toolbar to change its colour.

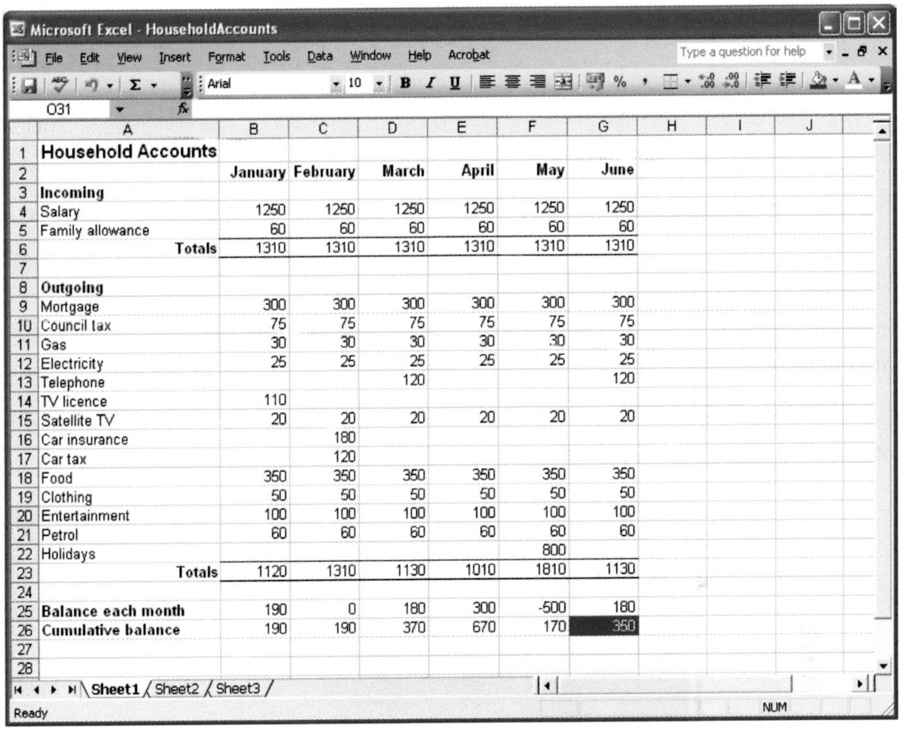

	A	B	C	D	E	F	G
1	Household Accounts						
2		January	February	March	April	May	June
3	Incoming						
4	Salary	1250	1250	1250	1250	1250	1250
5	Family allowance	60	60	60	60	60	60
6	Totals	1310	1310	1310	1310	1310	1310
7							
8	Outgoing						
9	Mortgage	300	300	300	300	300	300
10	Council tax	75	75	75	75	75	75
11	Gas	30	30	30	30	30	30
12	Electricity	25	25	25	25	25	25
13	Telephone			120			120
14	TV licence	110					
15	Satellite TV	20	20	20	20	20	20
16	Car insurance		180				
17	Car tax		120				
18	Food	350	350	350	350	350	350
19	Clothing	50	50	50	50	50	50
20	Entertainment	100	100	100	100	100	100
21	Petrol	60	60	60	60	60	60
22	Holidays					800	
23	Totals	1120	1310	1130	1010	1810	1130
24							
25	Balance each month	190	0	180	300	-500	180
26	Cumulative balance	190	190	370	670	170	350
27							
28							

Figure 6.17: The completed spreadsheet

What if?

Now you can use your spreadsheet to see how your financial situation would change under different circumstances.

- Try changing cells B20 to G20, setting each to 75, to see how much better off you would be at the end of the six months if you economised on your entertainment spending.
- What is the most expensive holiday you could afford? (Try increasing the value in cell F22 and watch your final balance in cell G26 approach zero.)

Surfing the Internet 7

Introduction to the World Wide Web

The Internet is made up of a huge number of computers – including yours – connected together, all over the world. By using the Internet you can look up information on any subject you can imagine, or send and receive messages through e-mail.

In this chapter we will concentrate on surfing the World Wide Web – the fastest-growing area of the Internet, made up of millions of web sites.

Every web site consists of one or more documents, called pages. A home page is the first page of a web site, which serves as an introduction to the rest of the contents.

WWF-UK: Homepage - Microsoft Internet Explorer
File Edit View Favorites Tools Help
Back Forward Stop Refresh Home Search Favorites Media History Mail Print
Address http://www.wwf.org.uk/core/index.asp
Go
WWF
Taking action for a living planet
WWF is best known for its work to conserve endangered species but we also endeavour to protec people and nature against threats such as climate change and the use of toxic chemicals.
Other WWF-UK sites
Search WWF-UK
find
About WWF
Take action
Wildlife
News
WWF-UK
Wednesday 14 August 2002
Take action: sign our petition
We want to change current legislation to increase the maximum sentence for illegal wildlife trade in the UK from two to five years, making this an arrestable offence. You can help us achieve this by adding your name to our online petition to the government. Add your name now.
Adopt an animal
WALK for WILDLIFE 2002
Contact us
WWF-UK
Panda House, Weyside Park
Godalming, Surrey GU7 1XR
t: 01483 426444
f: 01483 426409
e-mail us
Map and directions
Flick the switch on climate change
Climate change is possibly the most serious threat to our environment today, and we all personally contribute to this problem through our use of energy. You can help make a difference by contributing to the government's public consultation on what kind of energy will power the UK in the future. Take action now.
Wild Guesses
STOP ILLEGAL WILDLIFE TRADE
Action needed to prevent freshwater crisis
A new WWF report reveals that the Earth's most vital resource,
Ross Burden, celebrity chef
"I support WWF because its
Internet

Figure 7.1: The WWF home page

Pages on the World Wide Web are different from the pages you find in books. A web page doesn't have a set page size, so it can be short or long. When you print one web page, you could end up with several pages of A4 paper. Also, instead of page numbers, every page on the Web has its own address, called a Uniform Resource Locator (or URL).

Getting Started

The program you use to surf the World Wide Web is called a browser, and one of the most popular is Microsoft Internet Explorer. To load it:

- Either double-click on the icon for Internet Explorer on your Desktop.
- Or click Start at bottom-left of the screen,select All Programs, and then click Internet Explorer.
- You may see a dialogue box asking you if you wish to connect. If so, click Connect. (You may have to enter a username and password provided by your ISP.) An Internet page will appear on your screen – probably the one that the manufacturer of your computer has set as a default.

Tip: An **ISP** – Internet Service Provider – is a company that connects you to the Internet. Examples include **Tiscali**, **AOL** and **BT**.

You can go to a different address by typing in a new URL.

- Click in the Address box at the top of the window – the text will be highlighted.

Figure 7.2

- Type in www.guardian.co.uk and click Go.

Now your screen should look something like the one below. This is the web site of the Guardian newspaper. You will obviously be looking at it on a different date, so different news will be displayed.

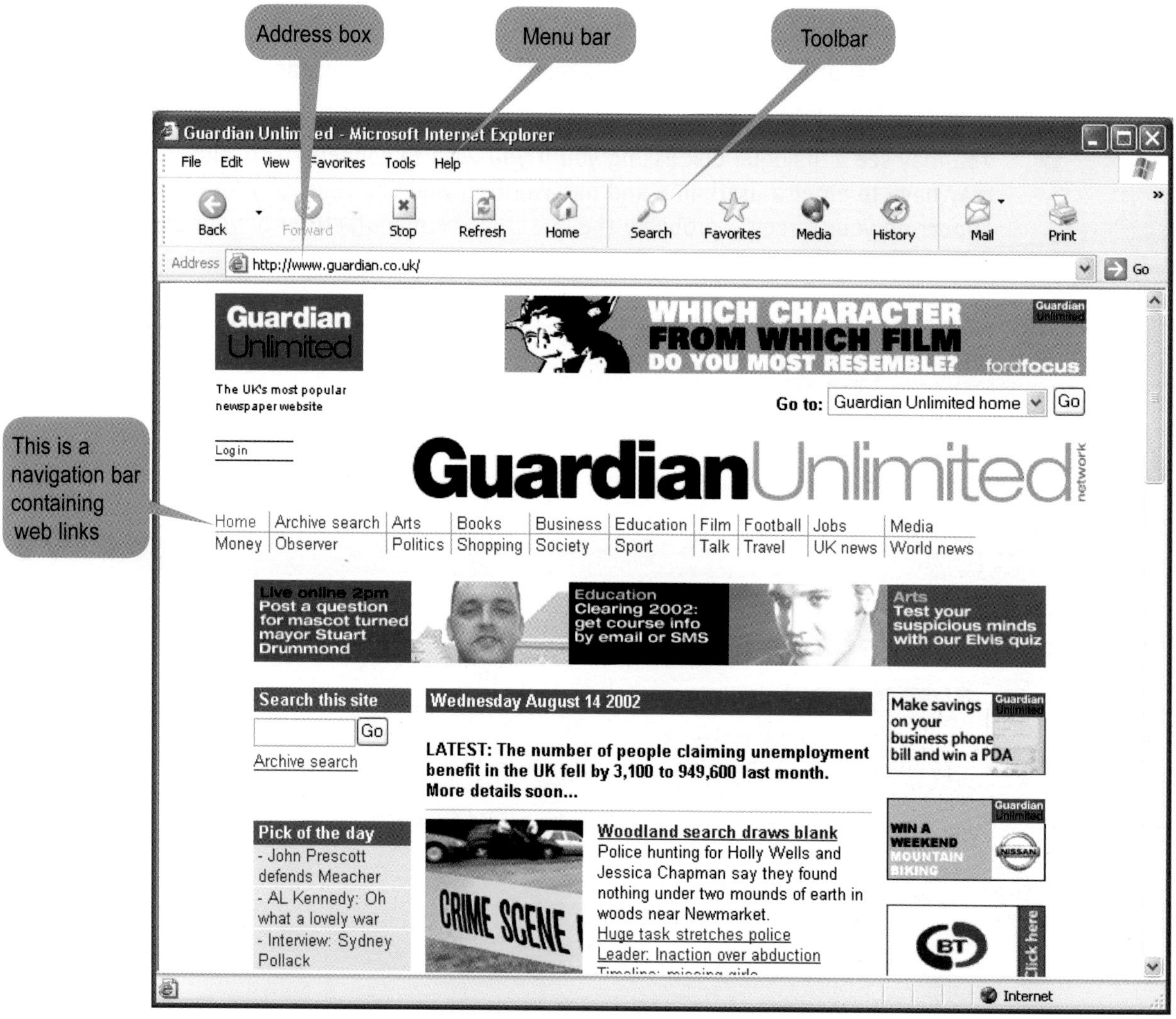

Figure 7.3

- To move about the web page, drag the scroll bar on the right side of the screen up and down.

- Web links (or hyperlinks) join pages together, and they often appear as underlined text. When your mouse pointer is on a link, the pointer turns into a hand. To move to another page, click a link with the left mouse button.

- Once you have followed a link, you can return to the previous page by pressing the Back button. You can then either choose a different link, or press the Forward button to retrace your steps.

Now practise accessing different web sites by typing in the URL of the site in the Address box and clicking Go. Also, follow some of the web links on the pages and use the Back and Forward buttons to move between pages.

- www.bbc.co.uk
- www.cocacola.com
- www.familyrecords.gov.uk
- www.louvre.fr

Note: When you visit these sites they may look different – organisations are constantly updating their web sites.

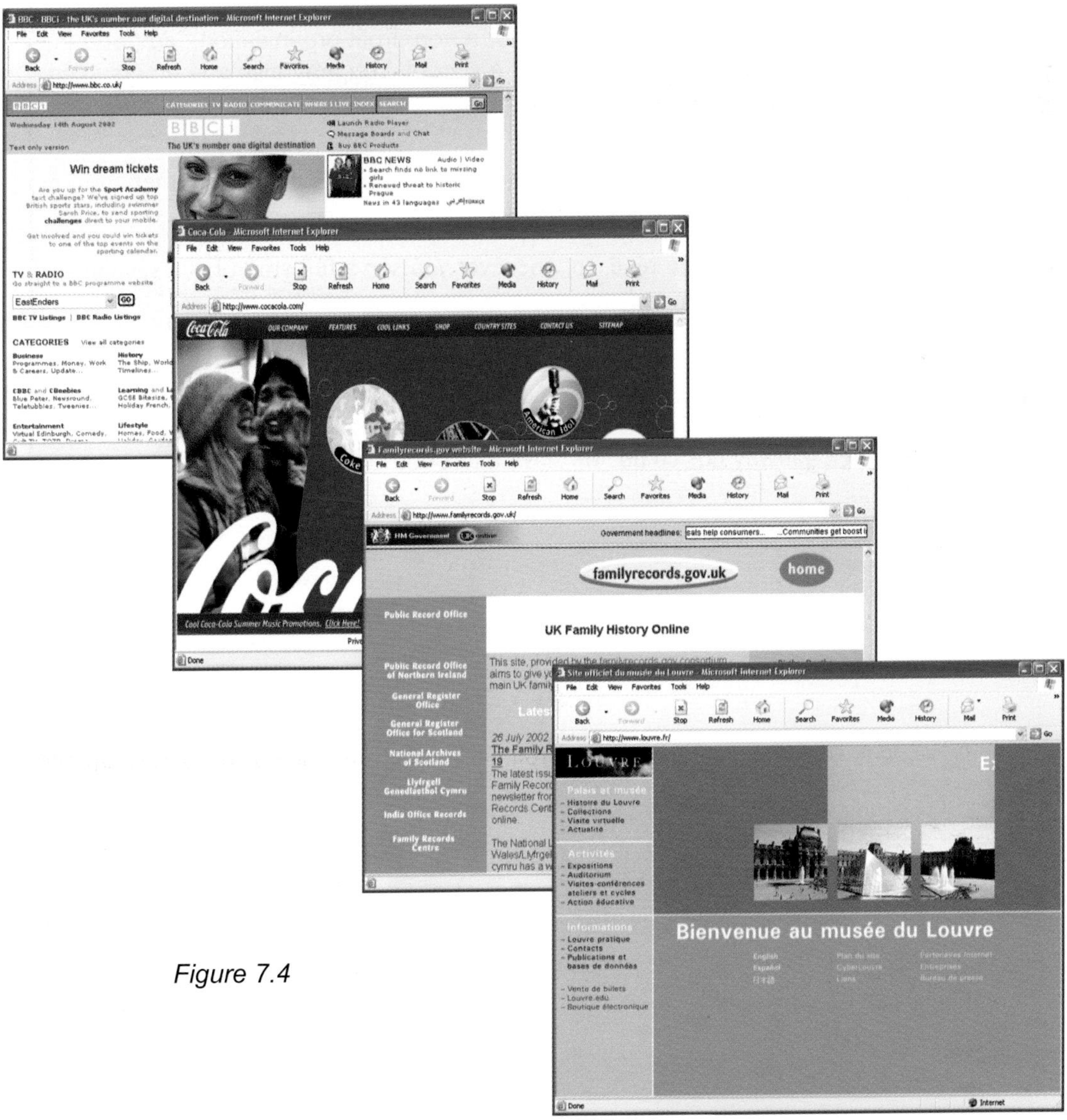

Figure 7.4

What's a domain name?

Every web page has a unique address, for example www.payne-gallway.co.uk/index.html

where:

www means World Wide Web and

payne-gallway.co.uk is the domain name. These have to be registered with a special Internet agency and then renewed (paid for) every few years to keep them active.

> **Tip:** The ending of a domain name can give you a clue as to the country or type of organisation that the URL belongs to.
>
> International companies often end their domains with **.com** and URLs ending in **.co.uk** usually mean a company from the United Kingdom. Some more examples of country codes are France **.fr**, Switzerland **.ch**, Germany **.de**, and Italy **.it**.
>
> Other codes include **.gov** for government, **.org** for a non-profit organisation, **.ac** (**.edu** in the USA) for a university or college and **.sch** for a school. You may also see others such as **.biz**, **.tv** and **.info**.

Index.html is the name of a specific page in the domain. Most pages end with either .html or .htm, although there are several other possibilities.

URLs are spoken just the way they're read, so whenever you see a full stop (.) you say dot and for a forward slash (/) you say slash.

For example:

www.payne-gallway.co.uk/index.html would be said out loud as

www dot payne hypen gallway dot co dot UK slash index dot html

Finding things on the Web

Finding web sites is easy enough when you know their web addresses, but what happens when you don't? Well that's when you need a search engine to help you out.

Search engines are a bit like reference libraries; they are powerful web sites that archive the content of the Web into searchable databases.

Search engines work in the same way as the database searches you might use in your local lending library: you type in a keyword or query and the site then returns a list of web sites containing your chosen word or phrase.

Tip: There are now over 550 billion documents on the Internet.

Examples include:

www.altavista.co.uk

www.lycos.co.uk

www.google.com

Let's use Google to find out the times of trains from Ipswich to London.

- In Internet Explorer type www.google.com in the address box and click Go.

You should see a screen something like the one below.

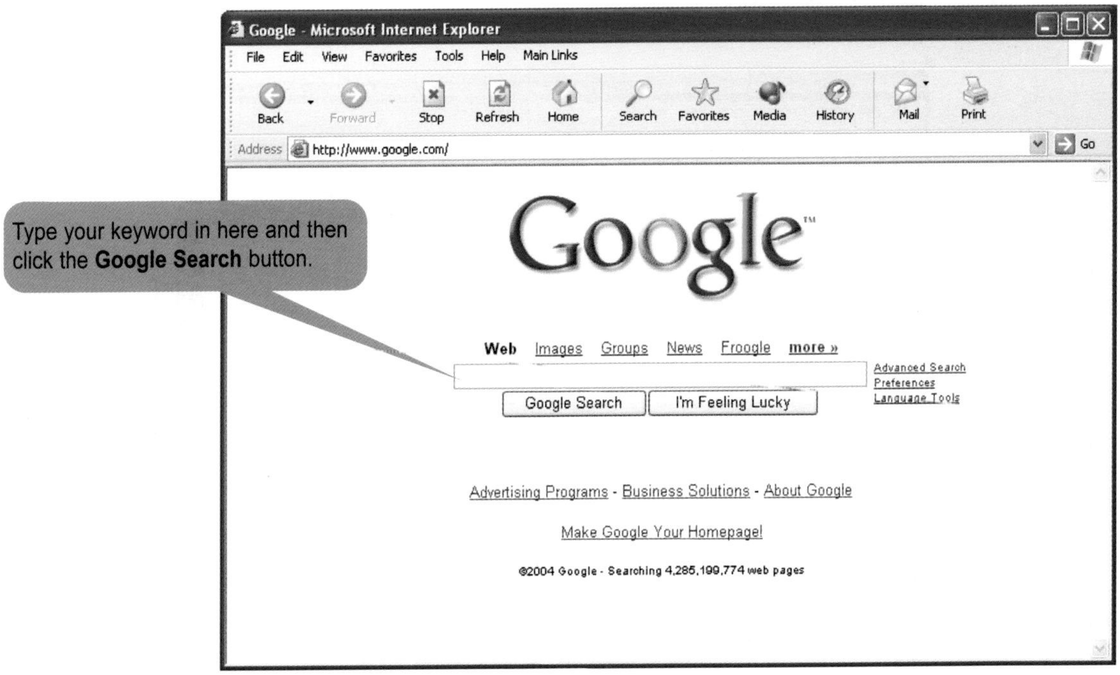

Figure 7.5

- Enter the text UK trains in the box and click the Google Search button.

A list of search results will be displayed.

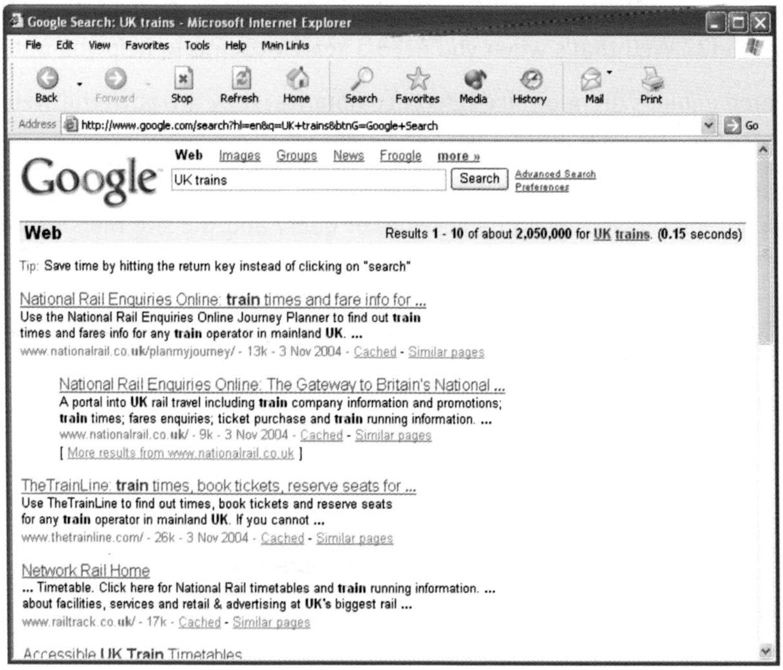

Figure 7.6

- Click on National Rail Enquiries Online and you will be taken to National Rail Enquiries.

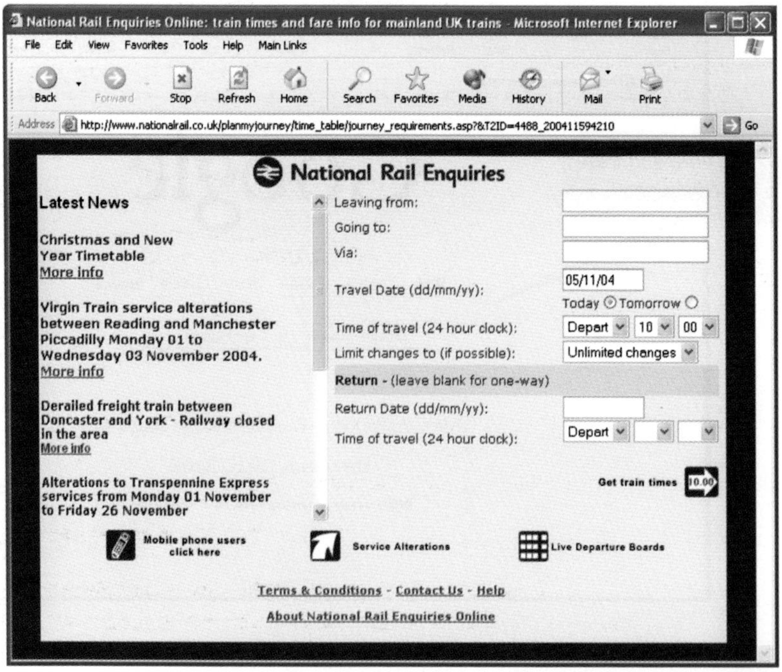

Figure 7.7

- Enter the details of your journey and click the Get train times button. The information you requested should be displayed.

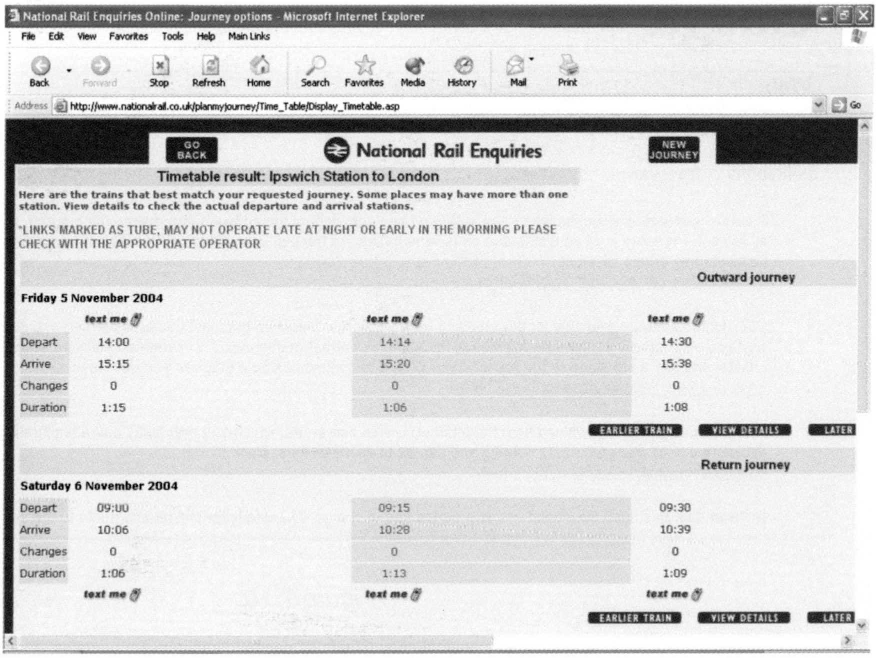

Figure 7.8

Google has lots of features to make searching for sites easier. Try some of these ideas.

- Do the same search again, but this time instead of clicking the Google Search button, click the I'm Feeling Lucky button. This takes you directly to the first web page Google returned for your query. You will not see the other search results at all – much quicker!

- To see a definition for a word or phrase, simply type define: and then the word(s) you want defined. If Google has seen a definition for the word or phrase on the Web, it will retrieve that information and display it at the top of your search results.

For example, to find a definition of the term freeware, simply type define:freeware into the search box and click the Google Search button.

Figure 7.9

You will be presented with various definitions and where they can be found.

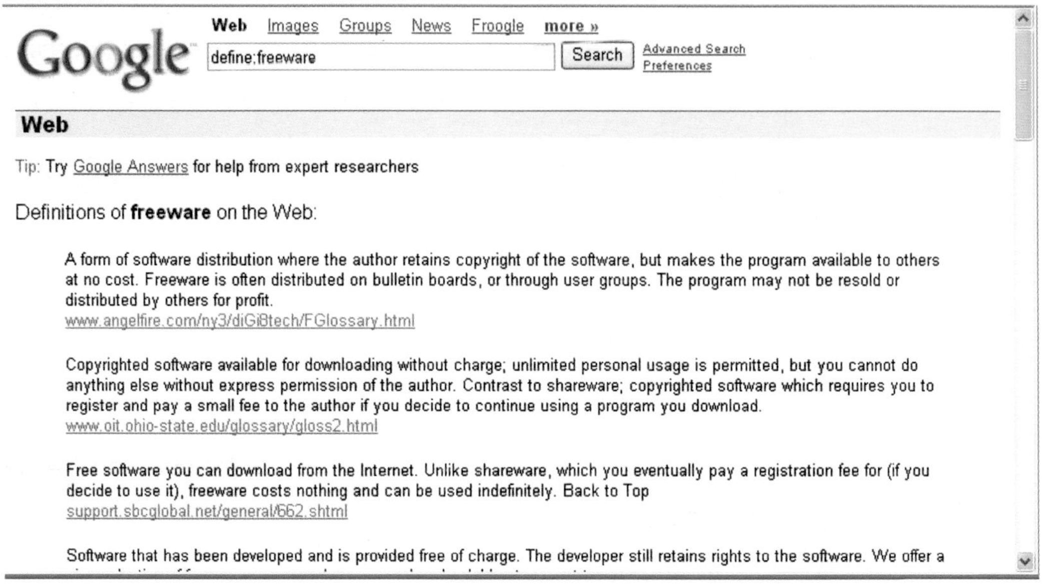
Google
Web Images Groups News Froogle more »
define:freeware
Search
Advanced Search
Preferences
Web
Tip: Try Google Answers for help from expert researchers
Definitions of freeware on the Web:
A form of software distribution where the author retains copyright of the software, but makes the program available to others at no cost. Freeware is often distributed on bulletin boards, or through user groups. The program may not be resold or distributed by others for profit.
www.angelfire.com/ny3/diGi8tech/FGlossary.html
Copyrighted software available for downloading without charge; unlimited personal usage is permitted, but you cannot do anything else without express permission of the author. Contrast to shareware; copyrighted software which requires you to register and pay a small fee to the author if you decide to continue using a program you download.
www.oit.ohio-state.edu/glossary/gloss2.html
Free software you can download from the Internet. Unlike shareware, which you eventually pay a registration fee for (if you decide to use it), freeware costs nothing and can be used indefinitely. Back to Top
support.sbcglobal.net/general/662.shtml
Software that has been developed and is provided free of charge. The developer still retains rights to the software. We offer a

Figure 7.10

- The word site followed by a colon enables you to restrict your search to a specific site. For example, to find information about the weather in Paris from the BBC web site type Paris weather site:www.bbc.co.uk and click the search button.
- To use Google's built-in calculator function, enter the calculation you'd like done into the search box and click on the Google Search button.

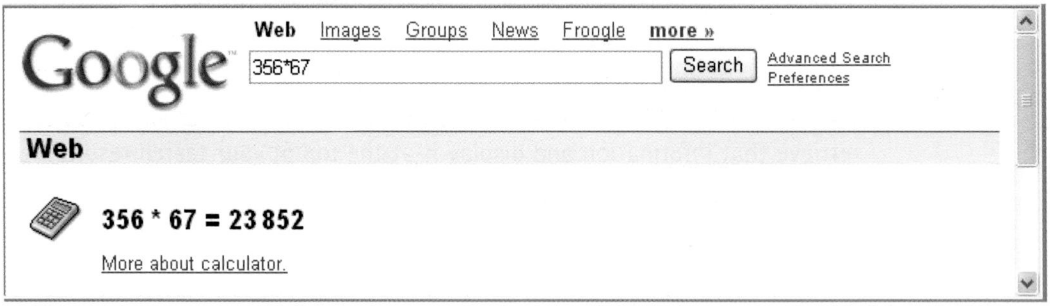
Google
Web Images Groups News Froogle more »
356*67
Search
Advanced Search
Preferences
Web
356 * 67 = 23852
More about calculator.

Figure 7.11

You can find lots more useful tips if you click on About Google on the Google home page (Figure 7.5).

Adding a bookmark

If you often have to travel by train to different destinations you might want to bookmark the timetables web page so that you can quickly access it again whenever you need to.

- Click the Back arrow to return you to the timetable search shown in Figure 7.7.

- Click the Favorites button on the Internet Explorer toolbar.
- In the window that appears click Add.

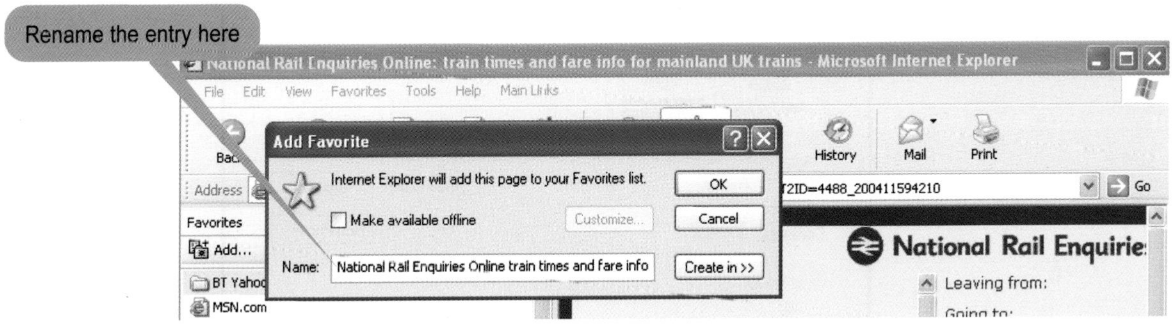

Figure 7.12

- In the Add Favorite box change the name if you wish and click OK.

The next time you want to look up a train timetable, simply click the Favorites button and a list of your favourite sites will be displayed in the left pane. You can choose the timetables web page from the list.

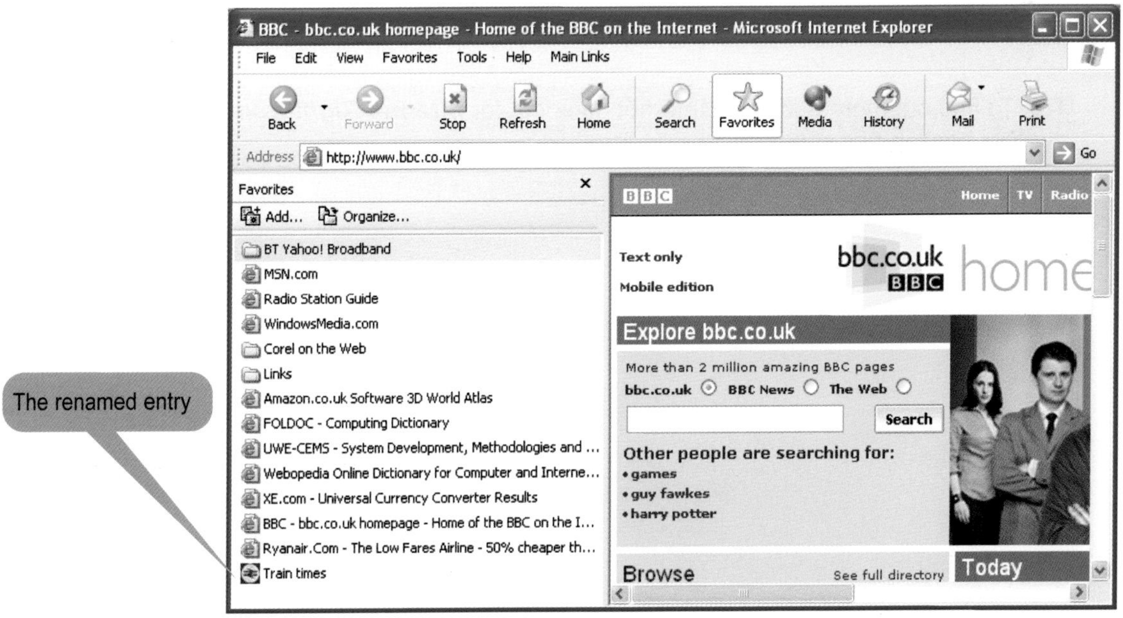

Figure 7.13: Choosing a page from Favorites

Printing a web page

Printing a copy of a web page onto paper is similar to printing a document you have created in a word processing package.

- With the timetable results page displayed on the screen select File, Print.

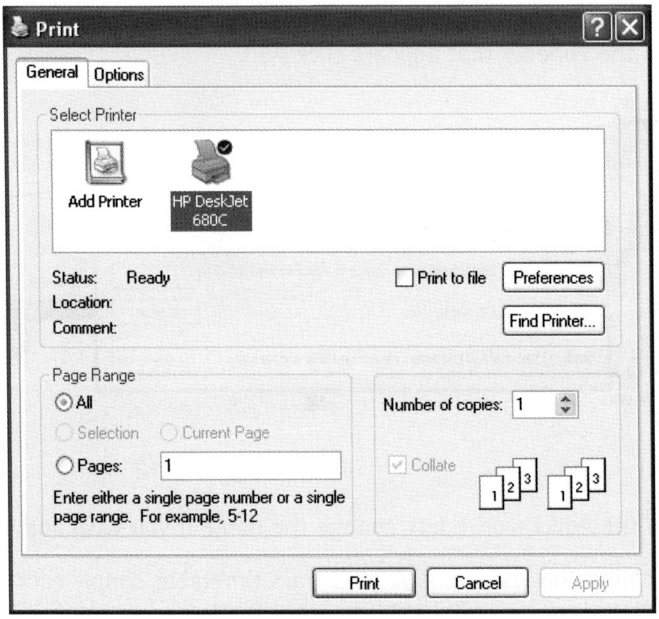

Figure 7.14

- Check the print options (in particular that Number of copies is 1) and then click Print.

> **Tip:** To find out more about the Internet, look out for ***Internet Right from the Start*** – another book in this series.

E-mails

8

Many people connect to the Internet so that they can send and receive e-mail. It has become one of the most popular forms of communication.

E-mail allows you to send a text message from your PC to anyone, anywhere in the world. It will arrive almost instantaneously and cost practically nothing.

There are two types of e-mail. The first is the kind of account you are given when you sign up with an ISP. To use this type of account you need a special program that allows you to connect to the Internet and collect your mail. One of the most popular ones is Outlook Express, which is supplied with the latest versions of Windows.

The second type of e-mail is called webmail. Instead of using a separate program to read and write your messages, you sign up for an account with a web site. You then have to log on to the Internet for all your e-mailing. One great advantage of webmail is that you can pick up your e-mails from any computer connected to the Internet. Examples of webmail sites include Hotmail (www.hotmail.com) and Yahoo! Mail (www.yahoo.com).

E-mail addresses

When you sign up for an e-mail account whether with a webmail service or with an ISP, you'll get your own unique e-mail address.

E-mail addresses are similar to web site addresses. They are always in this format:

username@domain_name

The username is the unique name you have chosen and domain name is that of the ISP or web mail site.

For example:

someone@hotmail.com

someone-else@tiscali.co.uk or

someone@payne-gallway.co.uk

Warning: You must enter an e-mail address correctly or the mail will come back undelivered.

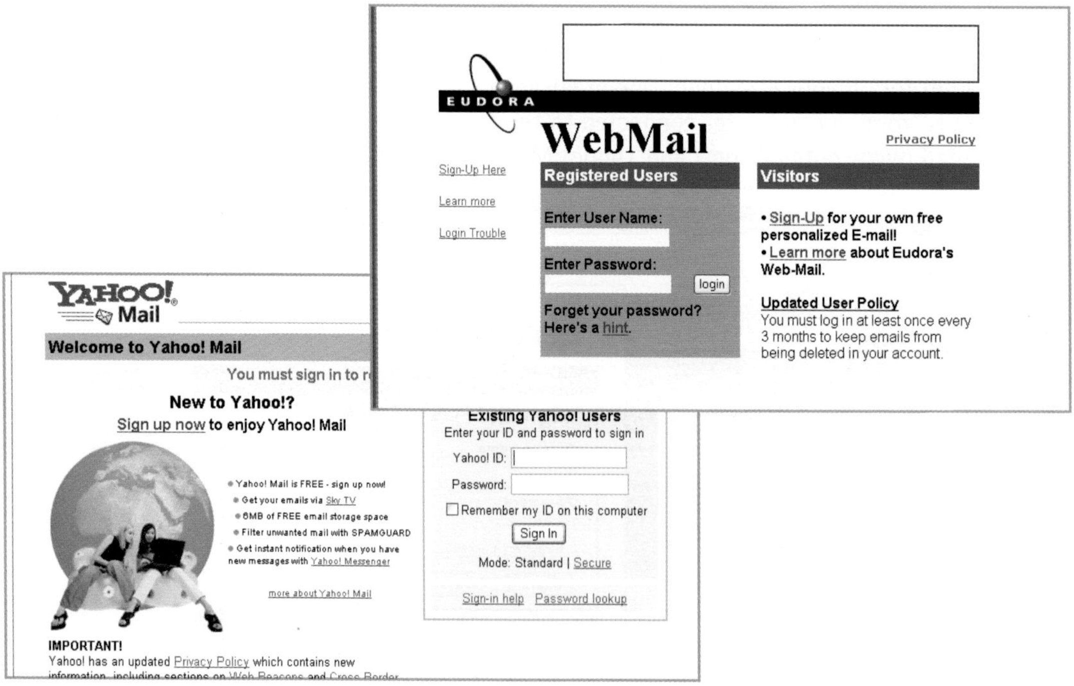

Setting up a Hotmail account

To use Hotmail you first have to register with them and choose a unique e-mail address.

- Log on to the web site www.hotmail.com. You will see a screen similar to this:

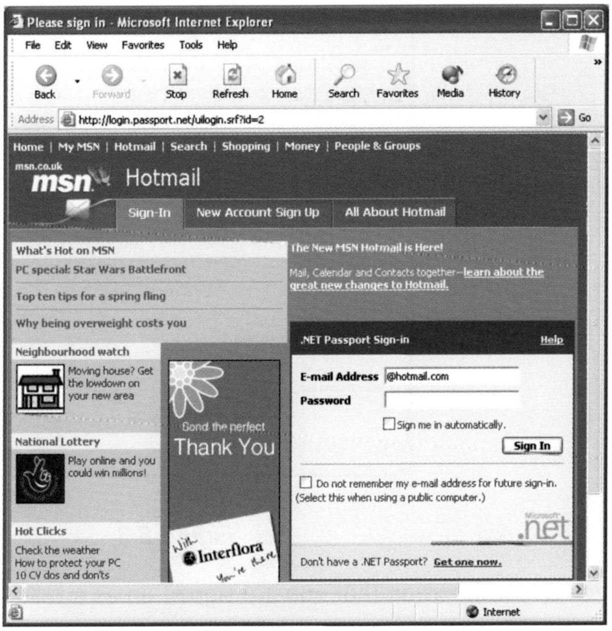

Figure 8.1

- Click on New Account Sign Up.

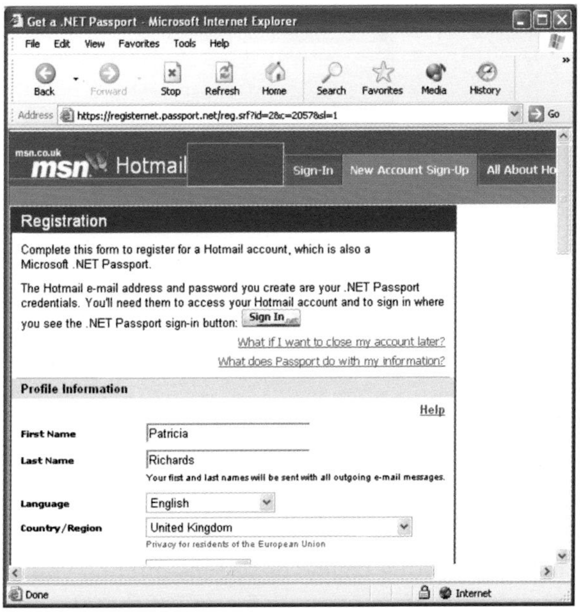

Figure 8.2

- Complete the registration form, giving the requested information.

If your chosen e-mail address is already being used by someone, you will be given some similar ones to choose from.

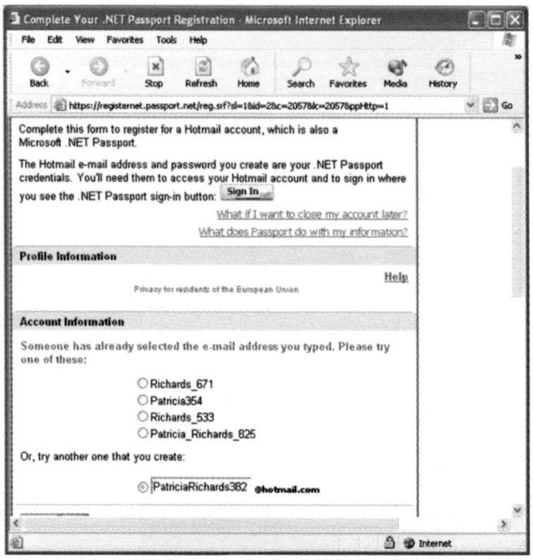
Complete Your .NET Passport Registration - Microsoft Internet Explorer
File Edit View Favorites Tools Help
Back Forward Stop Refresh Home Search Favorites Media History
Complete this form to register for a Hotmail account, which is also a Microsoft .NET Passport.
The Hotmail e-mail address and password you create are your .NET Passport credentials. You'll need them to access your Hotmail account and to sign in where you see the .NET Passport sign-in button:
Sign In
What if I want to close my account later?
What does Passport do with my information?
Profile Information
Help
Account Information
Someone has already selected the e-mail address you typed. Please try one of these:
Richards_671
Patricia354
Richards_533
Patricia_Richards_825
Or, try another one that you create:
PatriciaRichards382
@hotmail.com
Internet

Figure 8.3

You will receive confirmation that you are signed up as a Hotmail user.

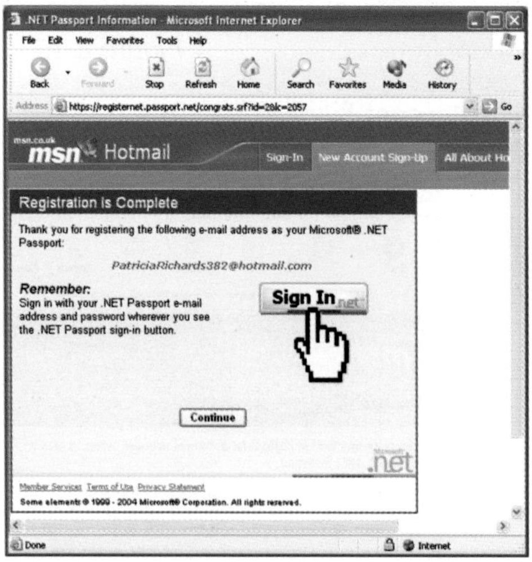
.NET Passport Information - Microsoft Internet Explorer
File Edit View Favorites Tools Help
Back Forward Stop Refresh Home Search Favorites Media History
msn Hotmail
Sign-In
New Account Sign-Up
Registration Is Complete
Thank you for registering the following e-mail address as your Microsoft® .NET Passport:
PatriciaRichards382@hotmail.com
Remember:
Sign in with your .NET Passport e-mail address and password wherever you see the .NET Passport sign-in button.
Sign In
Continue
.net
Done
Internet

Figure 8.4

- Click on Continue.
- Be sure to select Free E-mail on the next screen.

You will be presented with a couple of screens offering you newsletters and other promotional material – it's up to you if you sign up for any of these!

You will see the home page.

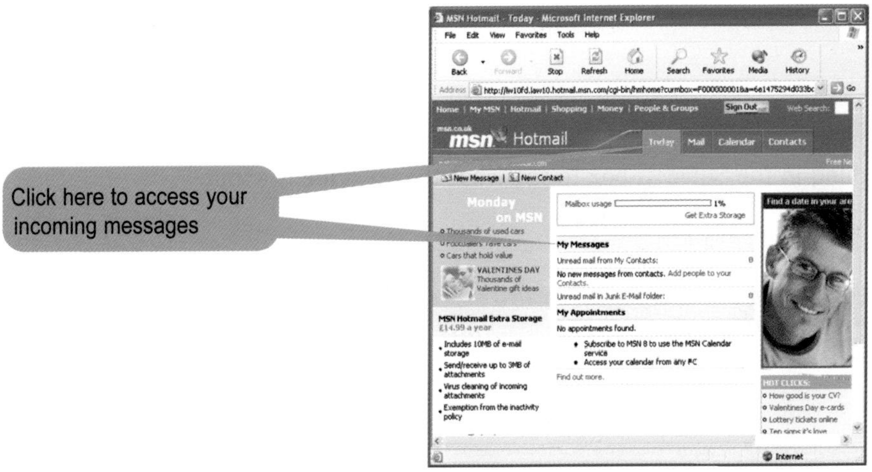

Figure 8.5

Tip: You will see lots of adverts – that's how they make their money!

Receiving messages

Incoming messages are stored in your Inbox. You will have received one message welcoming you to Hotmail.

- Click on either My Messages or the Mail tab (Figure 8.5).

A list of your messages will be displayed.

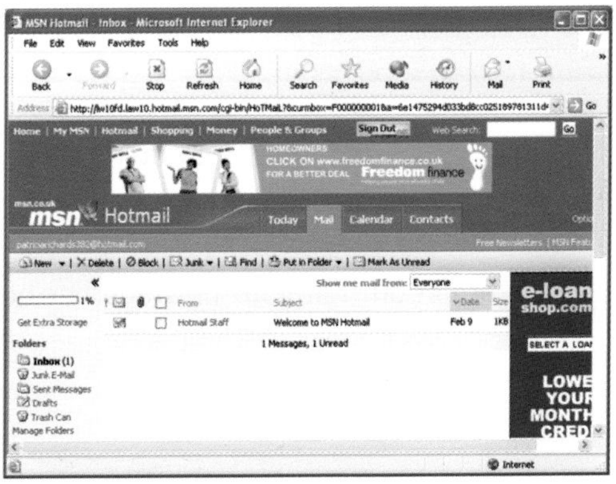

Figure 8.6: Accessing your messages

Warning: Watch out for spam – this is unsolicited junk mail. Never open these e-mails or their attachments, which often contain viruses.

- To read a message, click on the sender's name.

Sending messages

- Use the Back button to return to your messages (Figure 8.6).
- Click on New.
- Type the e-mail address you are sending to in the To: box.
- Type something in the Subject: box to say what the message is about.
- Type your message in the main window.

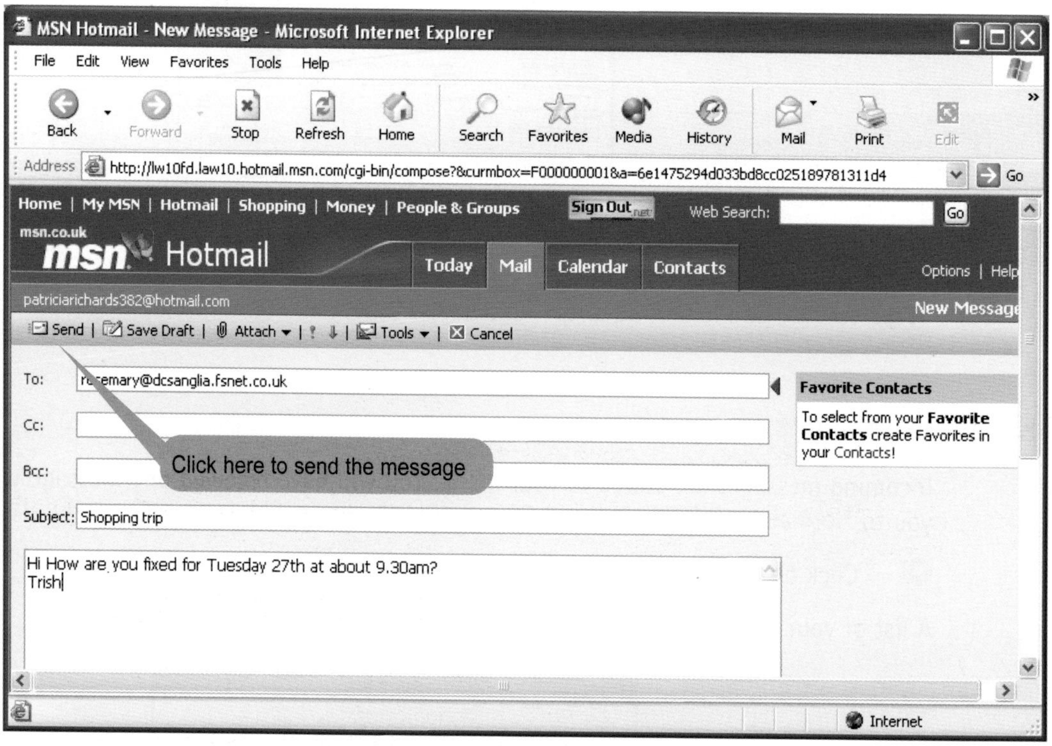

Figure 8.7: Sending a message

- Click the Send button.

You should receive confirmation that your message has been sent.

Using the Contacts list

The Contacts list stores the e-mail addresses of people that you regularly send e-mails to, so that you don't have to type in their addresses each time.

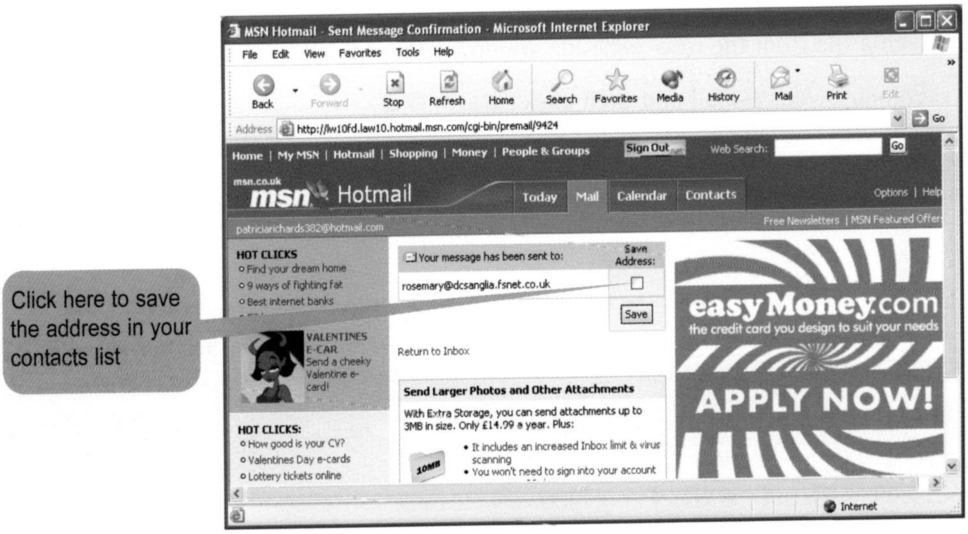

Figure 8.8

- Tick the Save Address box and click Save.

This will save the e-mail address as one of your regular contacts. You can assign it a short name to save you having to type in the whole address every time.

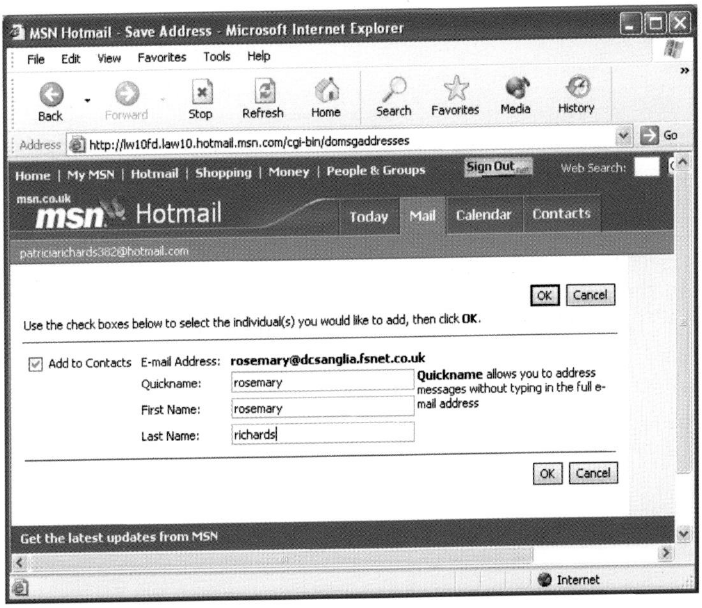

Figure 8.9

Sending an attachment

As well as the message you type into Hotmail you can attach one or more files to the email. You might want to attach a document that you have prepared in a word-processing or spreadsheet package, or perhaps a photograph you want to send to a relative.

You attach a file from the New Message window (Figure 8.10).

- Compose your e-mail and then click Attach, File.

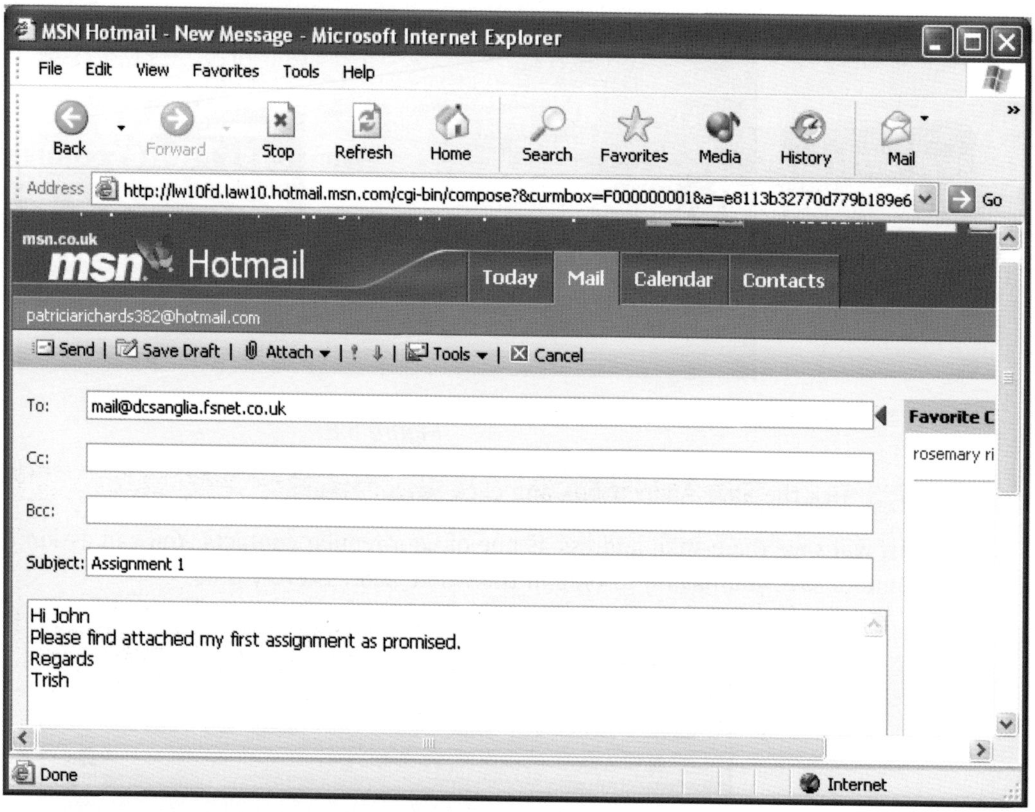

Figure 8.10

- In the next window, navigate to the file using the Browse button and then click OK.

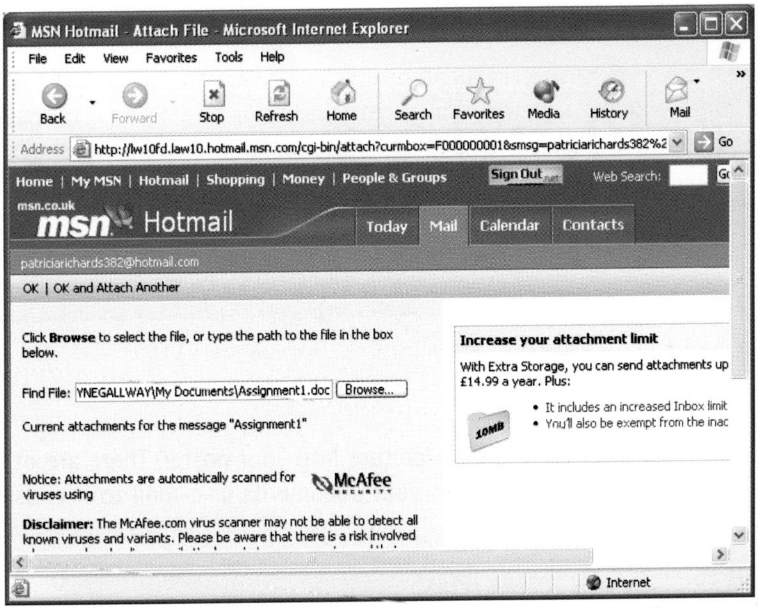

Figure 8.11

- When the file appears in the Attachments section, click Send.

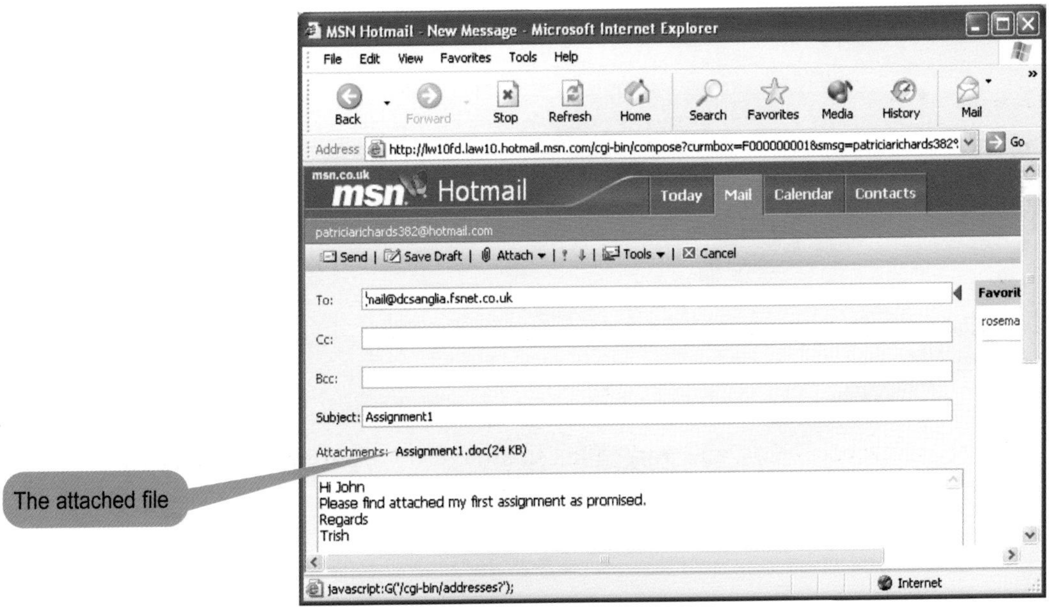

Figure 8.12: Sending an attachment

If you open a message that has an attachment, you will see the name of the attached file. Click on the file name to download it.

More Pictures

9

In Chapter 5 you inserted a clip art picture into your poster. There are other ways of acquiring pictures, which you can then use in your documents or e-mail to friends.

Scanning pictures

A scanner allows you to save a printed picture as a file on your PC. You can then print the picture, incorporate it into another document, use it on a web site or e-mail it to someone else.

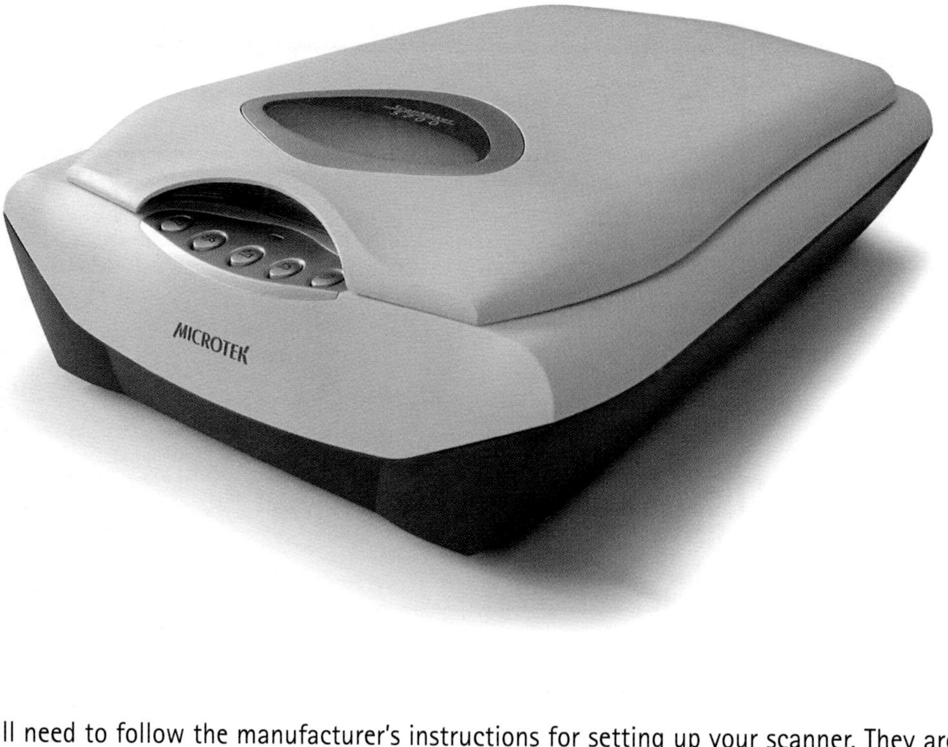

You will need to follow the manufacturer's instructions for setting up your scanner. They are all supplied with software that allows you to specify the type of image you want to scan, along with resolution (or quality) and colour settings. Some scanner software also allows you to edit the images you scan.

This example shows VistaScan software being used to scan a small area of a book cover.

- Load the scanner software program from the Start menu. You will see a screen with options similar to this.

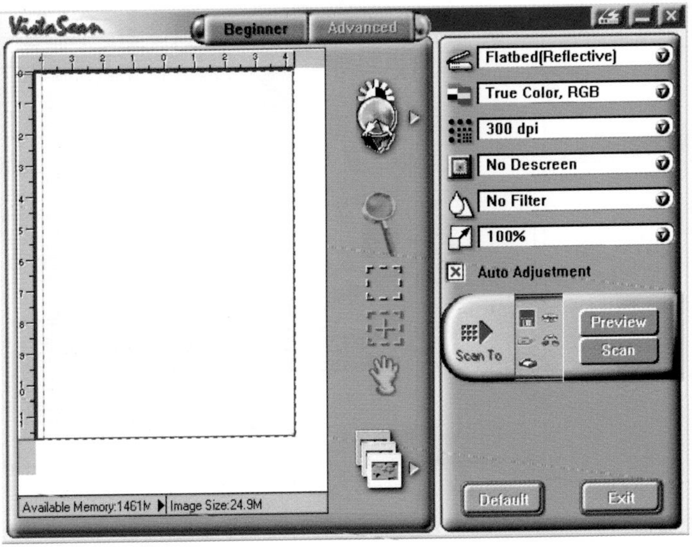

Figure 9.1

- Place the document to be scanned in the scanner and click on Preview. You will see the image on the screen.

Figure 9.2: Previewing the scan

- Use the mouse to drag the dotted lines around the area you want and click Scan.

You may be asked to specify where you want to save the image, or the software may default to a particular folder – make sure you know where the file is being saved.

Figure 9.3

Once the image has been scanned you can insert it into a Microsoft Word document.

- In a new Word document select Insert, Picture, From File.
- Find the scanned file and click Insert.

The image will be inserted into the document and you can size it as required.

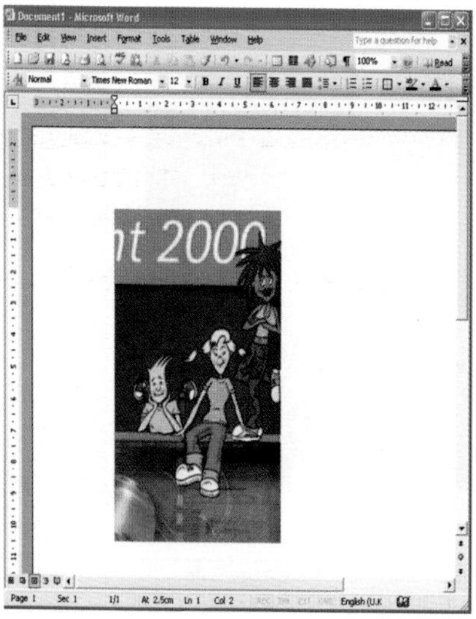

Figure 9.4: The scanned picture inserted into a Word document

Reminder: Look back at page 37 to remind yourself about sizing pictures.

Pictures from a digital camera

The main benefit of a digital camera is that you can transfer your photos directly to your PC without sending a film off to be developed.

Using a digital camera is very similar to using a traditional camera. They both use the basic components such as a lens, flash, shutter and viewfinder. Most digital models now incorporate an LCD screen so that you get a good of view of your subject as you take the photo, and you can then review the pictures afterwards.

The quality and number of digital pictures that can be taken will depend on the amount of memory in the camera.

Most digital cameras are now USB devices. This means that a cable supplied with the camera can connect it to a USB port on the back of your PC.

Tip: Universal Serial Bus (USB) ports are supplied on most desktop PCs. They can be used to connect different devices such as scanners, modems, printers and speakers.

To operate your camera you should refer to the manufacturer's instructions. When you have taken your photos and connected the camera to the PC a new 'virtual' drive will appear on your computer. Displaying the contents of this drive in My Computer will reveal a list of files.

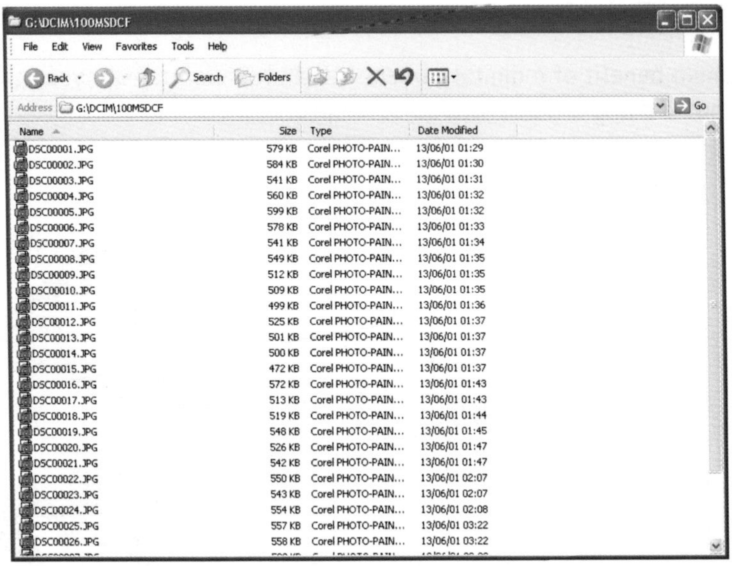

Figure 9.5

Tip: Unfortunately the pictures are not given very meaningful names.

To view the pictures, select Thumbnails from the Views button on the toolbar.

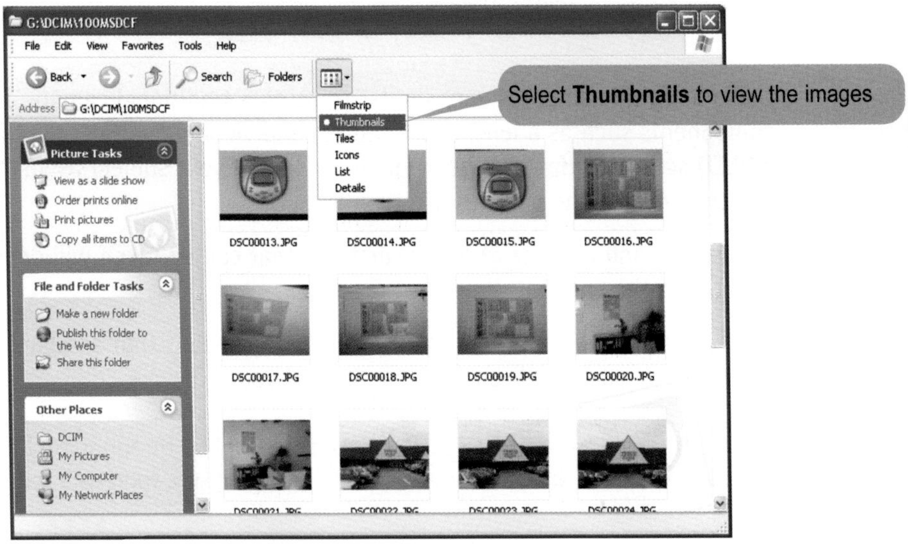

Figure 9.6: Viewing the digital pictures

You can then print these images, insert them into a Word document (as described in the previous section) or send them as e-mail attachment.s.

Reminder: Look back at page 74 to remind yourself about sending e-mail attachments.

Saving Internet pictures

Another limitless source of images is the Web. Follow these steps to save a picture.

- Log on to www.payne-gallway.co.uk
- To save the search engine graphic at the top-right of the home page, right-click it.

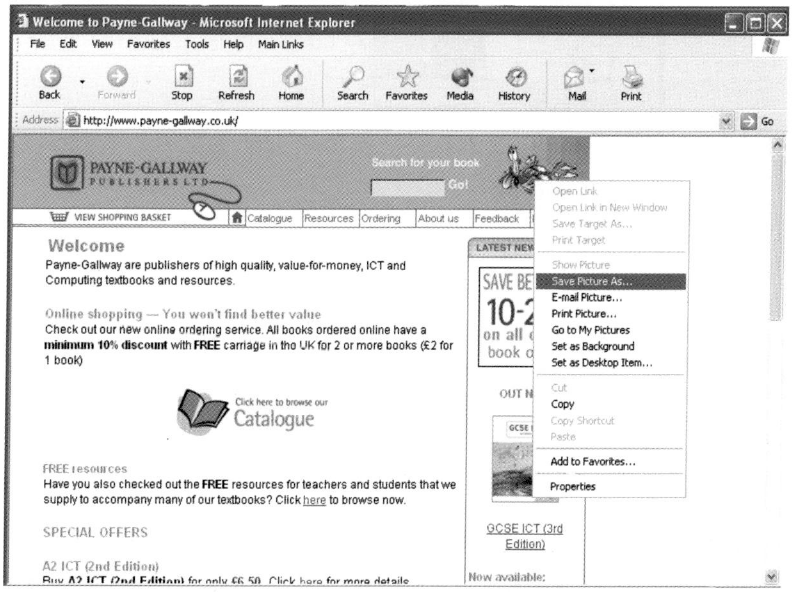

Figure 9.7

Warning: Always check the copyright status of pictures before you use them.

- From the menu that appears click on Save Picture As.

- In the Save Picture box, decide where you want to save the picture and give it a name.

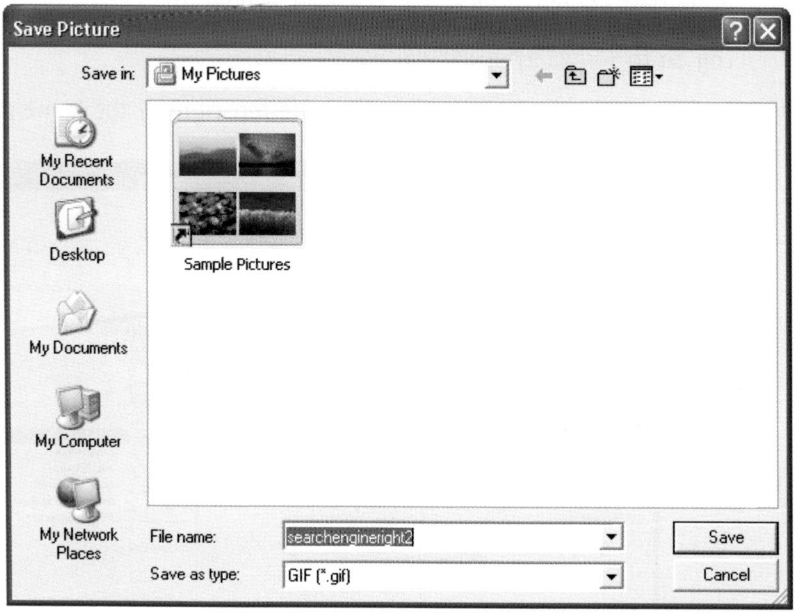
Save Picture
Save in:
My Pictures
My Recent Documents
Desktop
My Documents
My Computer
My Network Places
Sample Pictures
File name:
searchengineright2
Save as type:
GIF (*.gif)
Save
Cancel

Figure 9.8: Saving the picture

Reminder: Look back at previous chapters for details on e-mail attachments and inserting pictures in documents.

Now you can e-mail the picture, print it, or insert it into another document.

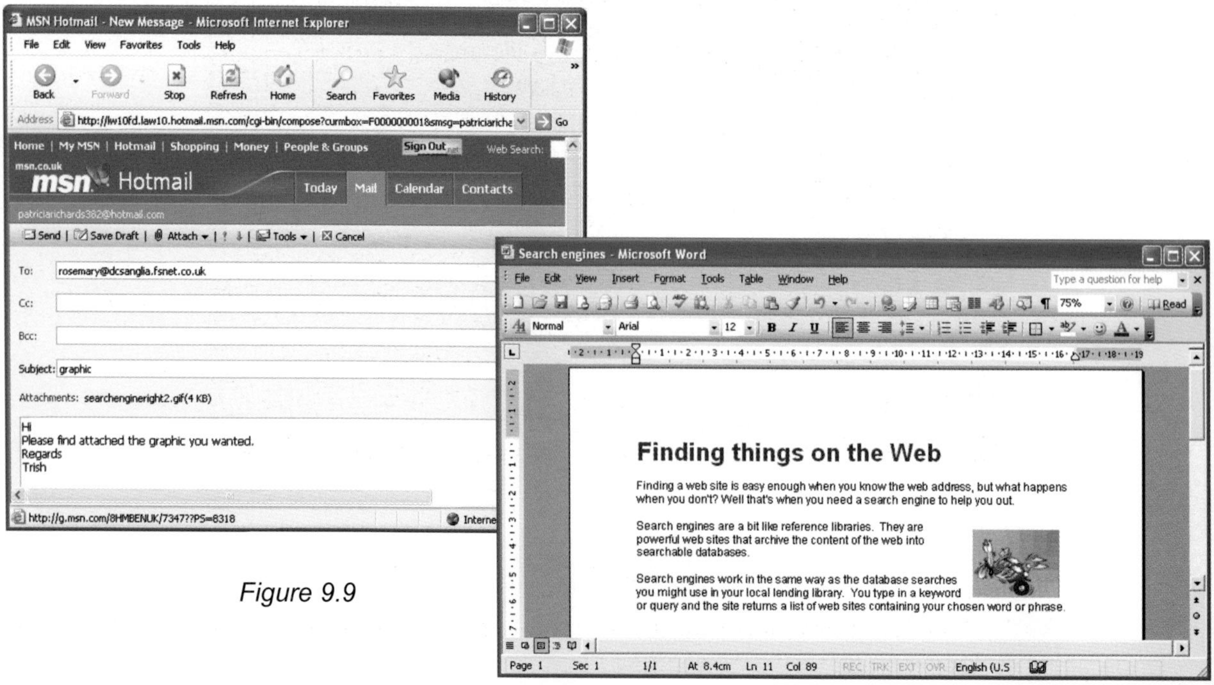
MSN Hotmail - New Message - Microsoft Internet Explorer
To: rosemary@dcsanglia.fsnet.co.uk
Subject: graphic
Attachments: searchengineright2.gif(4 KB)
Hi
Please find attached the graphic you wanted.
Regards
Trish
Search engines - Microsoft Word
Finding things on the Web
Finding a web site is easy enough when you know the web address, but what happens when you don't? Well that's when you need a search engine to help you out.
Search engines are a bit like reference libraries. They are powerful web sites that archive the content of the web into searchable databases.
Search engines work in the same way as the database searches you might use in your local lending library. You type in a keyword or query and the site returns a list of web sites containing your chosen word or phrase.

Figure 9.9

Music on the PC

10

Most computers are now capable of playing music: from a music CD, downloaded from the Internet or even music you record yourself.

Playing a music CD

- Insert a music CD into the CD drive of your PC.
- From the Start menu click All Programs.
- In the list of programs click Windows Media Player (supplied with Windows).
- Click on Play.

The music will start to play.

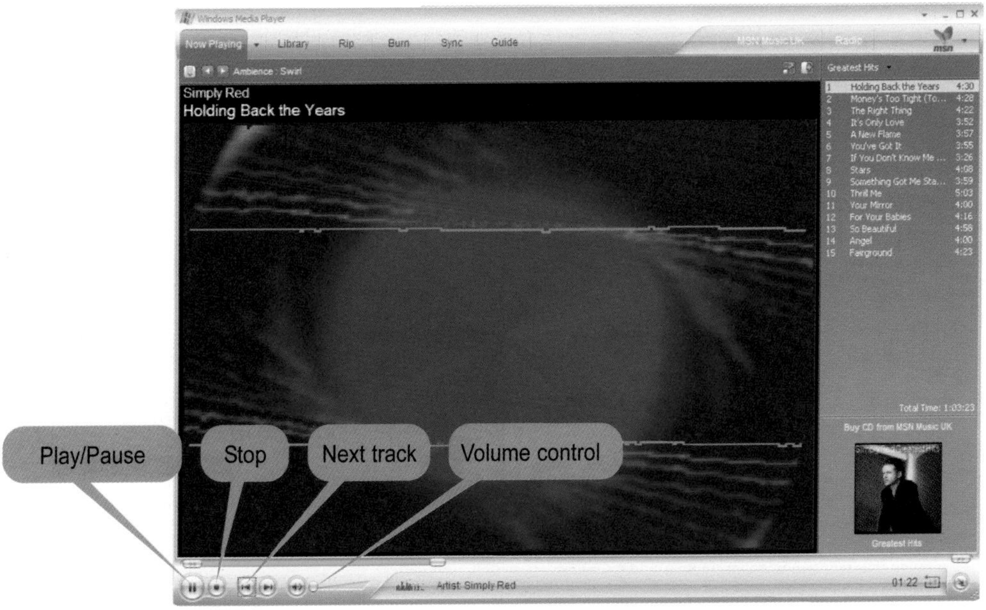

Figure 10.1: Playing a CD

Tip: If you are connected to the Internet and your CD is found in **Media Player's** online database, the CD information will be displayed.

- If you don't hear anything, check that your speakers are connected and switched on, and that the volume is high enough.

Downloading from the Internet

You can instantly boost your record collection by downloading music from the Internet. Music files are quite large, so they can take up a lot of space on your computer and take a long time to download from the Internet. Ideally you need to find Internet sites that have free MP3 downloads. MP3 is a technology that allows a music file to be compressed to a fraction of its original size.

You can try the site of your favourite artist or some of these:

www.mp3.com www.besonic.com

www.vitaminic.com www.emp3finder.com

Special programs are available to manage the music files you download and to play the music on your PC. However to begin with you can try playing the files using Windows Media Player.

- Log on to www.vitaminic.com

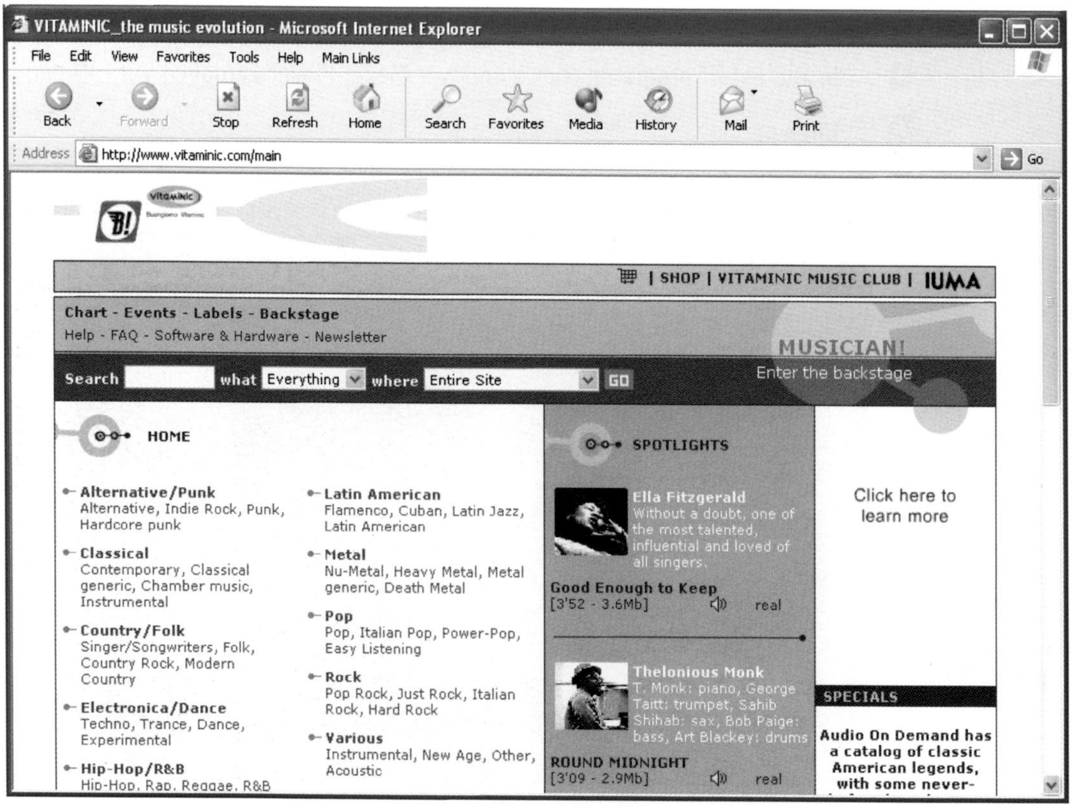

Figure 10.2

- Click on one of the music categories on the left or one of the Spotlights, for example Ella Fitzgerald in Figure 10.2.

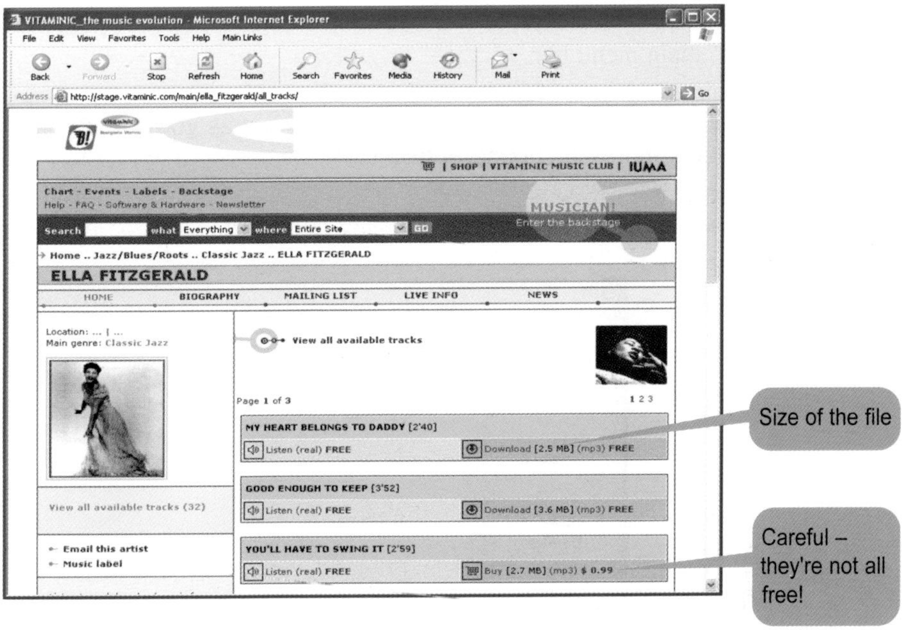

Figure 10.3

- Scroll down the list of songs and click on the one you want to download.

Windows Media Player will automatically open to prepare to play the music that is being downloaded.

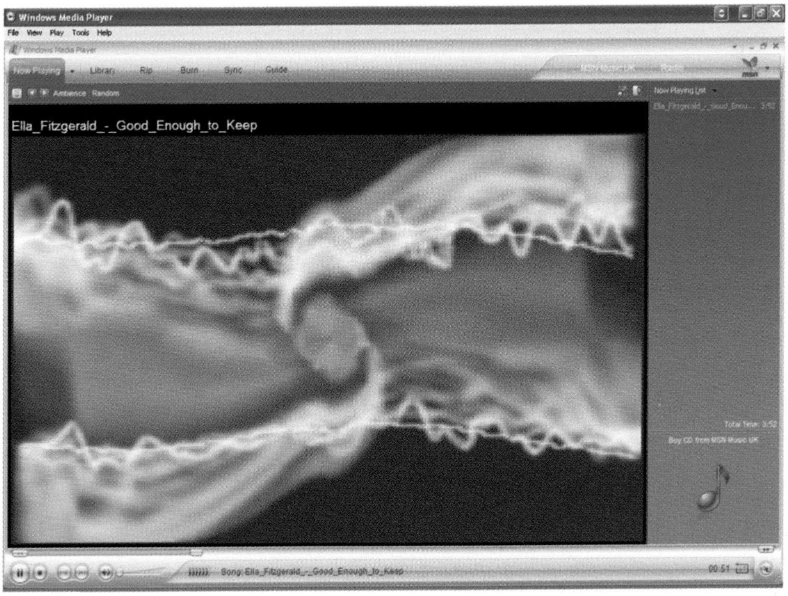

Figure 10.4

Tip: On some systems you will have to wait for the file to download before it begins to play.

- If you have enjoyed the track and would like to save it then select File, Save As from the main menu bar.

Tip: This may not be your taste in music, but as you can see this site has lots of different types of music to choose from.

A Save As dialogue box will appear inviting you to save the file in the My Music folder.

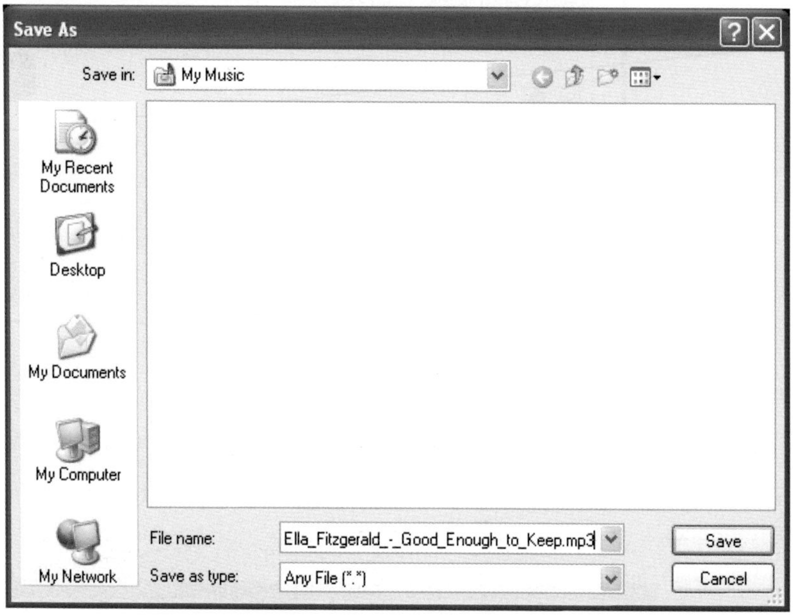

Figure 10.5: Saving the MP3 file

- Change the file name if you wish and then click Save.

When you want to play the track again, find the file in My Computer and double-click it. Media Player will automatically open and play the music.

Recording your own music

To record sounds using Microsoft Windows you need to connect an input device, such as a microphone or an electronic music keyboard, to your PC.

- Begin by checking that the device is not muted, by selecting Start, All Programs, Accessories, Entertainment, Volume Control.

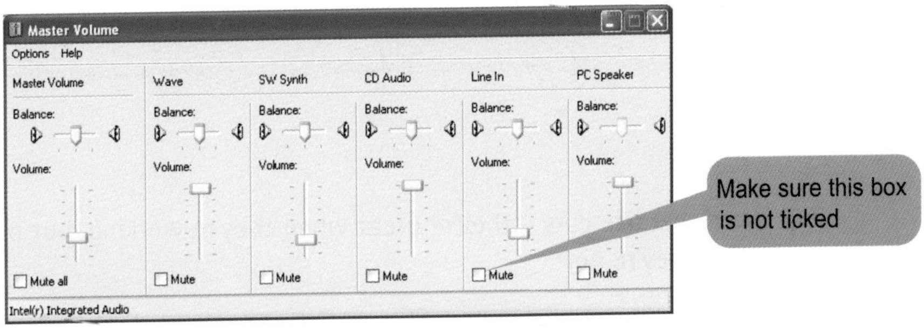

Figure 10.6

- Select Start, All Programs, Accessories, Entertainment, Sound Recorder.

Tip: There are other more sophisticated programs available for recording music.

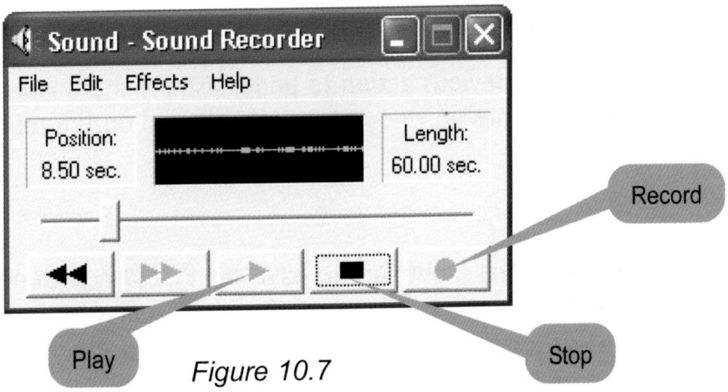

Figure 10.7

- Click the Record button and speak (or sing!) into the microphone.
- Click the Stop button and then click Play.

You should hear your voice being played back – if you've remembered to switch on the speakers!

- Use the Effects menu to increase or decrease the volume of your recording.
- Use the File menu to save your sound file.

Reminder: Try the **Help** menu if you want to find out more.

Troubleshooting

11

PCs are rather like cars – they're great when they're working, but oh boy can it be a problem to you when they're not!

It is surprising how quickly new PC users start to depend on their computer system, and how frustrating it can be when things go wrong.

In this chapter we look at some basic things you can try when you get a problem, and also some preventative measures you ought to take to stop the problems happening in the first place.

Using Undo

If you are creating a document and you do something wrong, don't panic. Most Windows programs will allow you to undo at least your last action. Some programs allow you to choose from a list which previous action to undo. Usually the Undo command is found in the Edit menu, and sometimes an Undo button is included on the toolbar.

Saving your work

It is a PC user's worst nightmare to have the PC crash with no warning in the middle of typing a long report. If you get into the habit of saving your work frequently, it will pay off in the end. Most Windows programs allow you to save your document quickly and easily by clicking the Save button on the toolbar.

Some programs also perform automatic saves at intervals that you can preset. If the computer crashes, the next time you load the program it will recover the document from the last automatic save it performed; this is called Autorecovery.

Switching off your computer

Before you switch off your computer you must close any programs that are open. You should then close down your computer from within Windows. If instead you just switch off your computer, it will not restart normally next time.

- When you have closed all your programs you should see only the Windows desktop on the screen.
- Select Start, Shut Down.

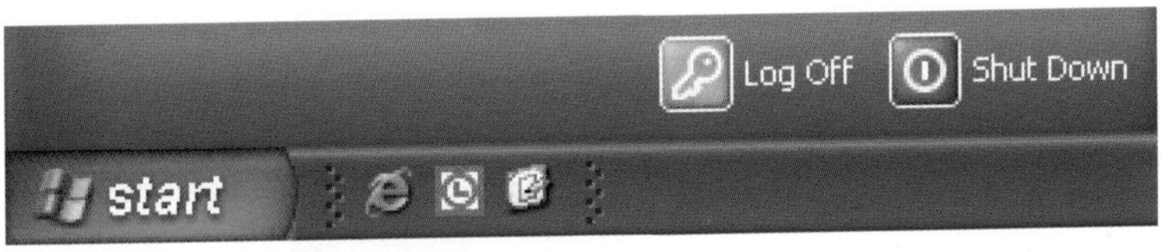

Figure 11.1

- In the box that appears click Turn Off.

Figure 11.2

- Wait for the screen to go black, or for a message to say that it is safe to turn off your computer.
- Power off the computer.

Tip: With Windows 2000 upwards, the PC switches itself off – but don't forget to turn the screen and printer off.

Finding files

Remember that you can search for files that you have previously saved, but now can't find. Use the search facility in My Computer (described in Chapter 3).

Retrieving deleted files

If you delete a file by mistake you will be able to retrieve it. All deleted items are removed to the Recycle Bin, although they will be deleted from there eventually. To retrieve a deleted file:

- Double-click the Recycle Bin icon on the Windows desktop.

Warning: Files deleted from a floppy disk are not sent to the Recycle Bin – they are lost forever!

You will see the following window:

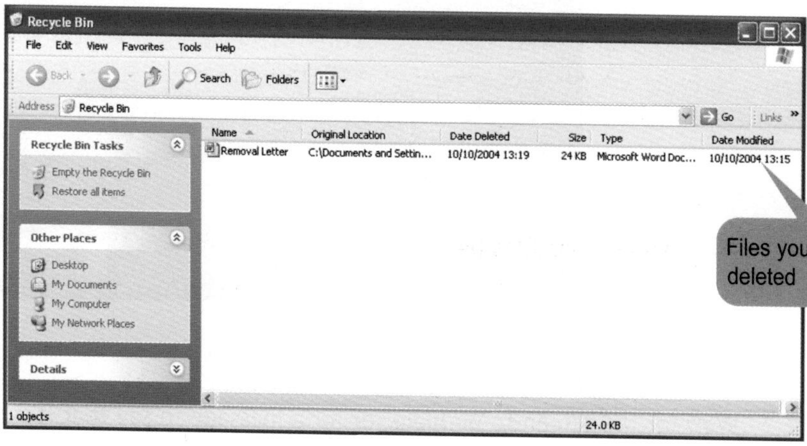

Figure 11.3: The contents of the Recycle Bin

The files that you have deleted are listed on the right-hand side.

- To restore a file, click it and select Restore this item from the Recycle Bin Tasks.

Although the files have been deleted, the Recycle Bin still takes up space on your hard disk drive. When it gets full it will automatically delete some of the oldest files, but it is a good idea to clean it out now and again.

- On the desktop right-click the Recycle Bin icon and select Empty Recycle Bin.

Figure 11.4

You will be asked if you are sure you want to delete the files.

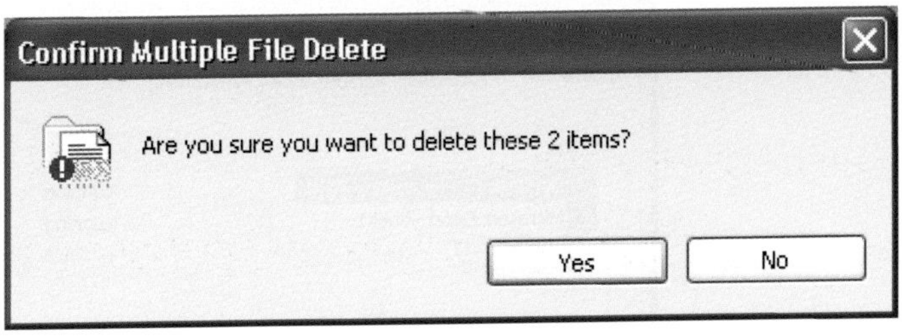

Figure 11.5

- Click Yes.

There's no getting those files back now!

If your PC crashes

Sometimes you might receive an error message before your PC stops working. If you're lucky this can help you identify the origin of the problem. However, often the error messages say something like You have performed an illegal operation, or a blue screen might appear telling you that there has been a Fatal exception error. These will probably leave you none the wiser. If you get these errors repeatedly, you will need to contact the manufacturer's technical support team. This is when you will be pleased that you purchased a support package with your PC.

If you get no response at all from your computer and are unable to shut it down in the proper way, only then as a last resort should you press the On/Off or Reset button. If you repeatedly do this it can damage your PC.

Restarting after a crash

If you have been unable to shut down your computer correctly, then when you restart the first thing it will do is to run a program called chkdisk (or Scandisk, depending on your version of Windows). This checks your hard disk for any damage. If the scan finds any problems it will tell you if they can be repaired.

If your screen freezes up

If you are working on your PC and it locks up so that you cannot use the keyboard or mouse, you can try to find out which program is causing the problem.

- Press Ctrl+Alt+Del on the keyboard (all at the same time).
- In the window that appears click Task Manager.

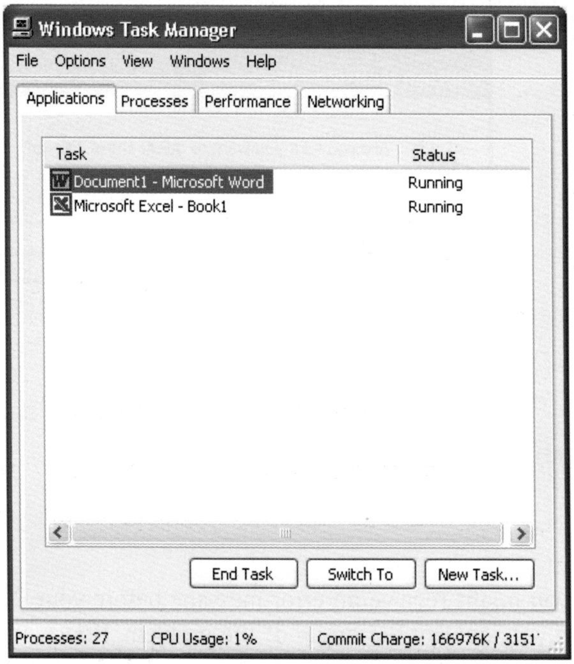

Figure 11.6: Task Manager

- Any program whose status is Not Responding may be at fault.
- Click the name of the program and click End Task to close it.

This should close down the faulty program and allow you to carry on working. If it doesn't, click Shut Down – this will close down your PC safely, and is always better than hitting the Reset button.

Virus Checking

Viruses are designed to create problems with your PC, or at least to cause you some inconvenience. At worst they can wipe all the data saved on your hard drive. All PCs should have virus-checking software installed. The package should be capable of scanning and clearing viruses from the system. As new viruses are being discovered regularly it is recommended you install a package, such as Norton AntiVirus, that provides an on-line update service.

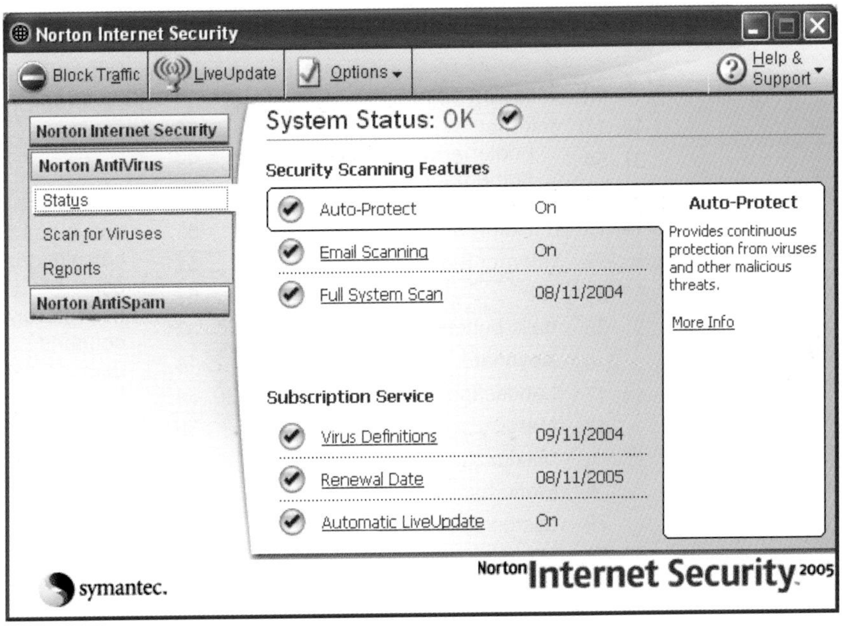

Figure 11.7: The Norton AntiVirus utility

The dramatic proliferation of viruses over recent years is due in part to e-mail communication.

Never open an e-mail attachment from someone that you don't recognise – it could well introduce a virus to your system.

So that's it – now you're ready to move on to some of the other books in this series!

Index

AutoSum 52
Backspace key 14, 17
Bold button 37, 54
Borders button 54
Caps Lock key 14, 15
CD-ROM 2
Center button 34
Clip art 36
Close button 7, 8
Delete key 14, 17
Deleting text 17
Desktop 3
  background 4
Digital camera 79
Domain name 60, 68
Drop-down menu 9
E-mails 67
  address 68
  attachment 74
  Contacts list 73
  Inbox 71
  receiving messages 71
  sending messages 72
Enter key 14, 15, 17
Favorites button 65
Files 19
  copying, deleting, moving 23
  searching for 26
Fill Color button 55
Fill handle 45, 50, 52, 53
Floppy disk 2
Folders 19
  copying 23
  creating 20
  deleting 23
  moving 23
Font Color button 40, 55
Google 61
Hard disk 2
Help 11
Hotmail 67
Icons 3
Insertion point 14
Internet 56
  bookmark 65
  home page 56
  hyperlinks 58
  pictures 81
Internet Explorer 57
ISP 57
Italic button 37
Keyboard 2, 14
Landscape orientation 30, 34
Margins 39
Maximize button 7, 8
Menu bar 8, 13, 44
Microsoft Excel 2003 42
Minimize button 7
Mouse 2, 5
  pointer 6, 16
  practice 6
MP3 downloads 84
Music 83
  downloading 84
  recording 87
My Computer 20
My Documents 19
Outlook Express 67
Page Setup 29, 34, 39
PC crashes 91
Pictures 36, 76
  inserting 36
Portrait orientation 30
Print Preview 31, 38
Printer 2
Printing 28
Recycle bin 90
Save button 31, 38
Saving 19, 51, 88
Scanning pictures 76
Screen 2
Scrolling 4, 18
Search engine 61
Shift key 14, 15
Shut down 89
Space bar 14, 17
Speakers 2
Spreadsheet 42
  active cell 44
  calculations 52
  cell 44
  cell reference 44, 52
  columns 44
  deleting data 47
  formula bar 46
  formulae 52
  inserting and deleting
    columns and rows 49
  rows 44
  SUM function 53
Start menu 6, 8, 12, 43
System unit 2
Tab key 14, 37
Task bar 8
Task Manager 92
Task pane 13, 43
Text 34
  alignment 34, 54
  selected 17, 35
  size 35, 54
  style 40
Title bar 7, 13
Troubleshooting 88
Undo 35, 47, 49, 88
Uniform Resource Locator (URL) 56
USB 79
Virus checking 93
Web links 58
Web pages 56
  printing 66
Web sites 56
Webmail 67
Windows Media Player 83
Word processing 12
World Wide Web (www) 56